NEXT OF KIN

An important, compassionate and practical guide that we are all likely to need at some stage given the inevitability of losing someone we love.

—**Dr Preeya Alexander, GP**

Next of Kin doesn't sugarcoat it. You'll feel less alone—and walk away with straight-up, practical ways to make the most of the time you've got, and hold on tight to the memories when that time's up. Nothing can replace that.

—**Ryan Bowles,** *Good Grief*

An excellent guide to the unique challenges we face when we need to step up as Next of Kin. I wish I had this book before my father became ill and died. *Next of Kin* offers crucial life skills wrapped up in a warm and touching story of Casey's own life experience. A great read and so valuable.

—**Karen Carey, Consumer advocate**

Both tender and fearless, *Next of Kin* is a lighthouse in the storm of care, loss and grief—steady, human, honest, and impossibly kind. The chaos, the heartbreak, the absurd moments; it holds your hand through it all.

—**Dr Gina Cleo, PhD, founding director,**
Habit Change Institute

This is a rare find. There is no rule book when it comes to caring for a loved one, but Next of Kin is the guide that every carer should have. It's a lifeline that offers not only knowledge, but comfort, humanity and a sense of community in a time where most feel very alone. A must-read.

—**Ellie Cole, AM**

As someone who has seen firsthand the immense challenges and emotional weight that come with caregiving, I cannot overstate how important *Next of Kin* is for those navigating the complex and often overwhelming health care systems. Casey's deeply personal journey with her father's illness speaks to a universal truth—carers are the unsung heroes of society. This book not only provides practical advice, but it also offers the compassion, understanding, and guidance that every carer needs to feel empowered, supported, and less alone.

Next of Kin is a must-read for anyone juggling the responsibilities of caring for an aging parent while balancing their own life. Casey's approach is both empathetic and insightful, giving readers the tools to advocate for themselves and their loved ones with dignity. This is the resource I wish I had when my own family faced difficult health challenges. I am proud to support Casey and her incredible work in sharing this vital resource with the world."

—Barry Du Bois, TV legend

This book is a must read for anyone caring for a loved one, or anyone dealing with grief and loss. Which makes it a book for all of us. I felt reading this as if I were being enveloped in a big warm hug by a friend helping me navigate the inevitable pain that life brings. Absolutely dripping with empathy and understanding as well as practical and sound advice. A wonderful book about something very difficult. Thank you Casey for writing it, and for caring for your Dad with such grace and humility.

—Dr Sonia Henry, GP

Casey is a thoughtful and compassionate interviewer and these same values leap off of every page in this book. If only I had this much needed guide when I was losing my beautiful Mumma. In true Casey form she reminds us we can do hard things while also understanding the need to fall apart. I have no doubt this will help so many others through loss and life.

—Samantha Jade, singing superstar

I needed this book 2 years ago, I need it now and I am certainly going to need it in the future. We all will. I have watched Casey navigate this topic as she cared for my dear friend and her father, Jack. She is brave and stoic at the same time as human and enormously generous. This book takes all that experience and emotion and delivers it to us in an approachable and companionly way. It's a generous work and I am grateful to Casey for living it so well and sharing it with us.

—Luc Longley AM, NBA Superstar

Next of Kin invites you into one of life's hardest but most beautiful chapters. With equal parts humour and humanity, this book goes where so few dare to, even traversing the financial, emotional and spiritual costs of care. It's like *The Barefoot Investor* for carers, every house needs a copy.

—Lisa Messenger, CEO, Collective Hub

We don't talk about death enough. Or grief. This book gives us the language to tackle the stuff we'd prefer to avoid. Casey writes with guts, humour and honesty—and reminds us we're not alone in the hard stuff.

—Turia Pitt, runner, mum, coach, and occasional *Hard Quiz* answer

Although we, as a society, have become a bit better about talking about 'not being OK', discussions about death and dying and all that comes with it are still few and far between. It's not surprising we avoid difficult conversations, but thankfully Casey has now given us all a roadmap to navigate these distressing periods in life. *Next of Kin* is powerful and practical, and I've no doubt it will be beneficial to many, many people.

—Dr Tim Sharp, The Happiness Institute

This book will have you laughing, crying and deeply contemplating life's most pivotal and challenging moments all at once. Through the perfect mix of lived experience and practical advice, this candid, informative and insightful work will hold your hand through the loneliest of roads. This is a book everyone needs to read, not just for themselves but for those they love.

—Dr Michela Sorensen, GP

Part permission slip, part prayer, part instruction manual. I'll be pressing this into friends' hands for years.

—**Sean Szeps, Digital Dad**

In Next of Kin, Casey Beros has created something rare and vital—a brutally honest, tender, and deeply human guide for what it means to walk alongside someone you love at the end of their life. With equal parts grit, grace, and humour, she offers not just practical wisdom, but emotional companionship—the kind you crave when the ground falls out from under you. This book is a light in the dark, a steady hand on your back, and a reminder that while the path of caregiving and grief may be messy and painful, we don't have to walk it alone.

—**Dr Shoshana Ungerleider, medical doctor, founder of End Well**

NEXT OF KIN

WHAT TO EXPECT WHEN YOU'RE EXPECTING
TO CARE FOR SOMEONE YOU LOVE

CASEY BEROS

WILEY

First published 2025 by John Wiley & Sons Australia, Ltd

ISBN: 978-1-394-33797-2

A catalogue record for this
book is available from the
National Library of Australia

Registered Office
John Wiley & Sons Australia, Ltd. Level 4, 600 Bourke Street, Melbourne, VIC 3000, Australia

For details of our global editorial offices, customer services, and more information about Wiley products visit us at www.wiley.com.

Wiley also publishes its books in a variety of electronic formats and by print-on-demand. Some content that appears in standard print versions of this book may not be available in other formats.

Trademarks: Wiley and the Wiley logo are trademarks or registered trademarks of John Wiley & Sons, Inc. and/or its affiliates in the United States and other countries and may not be used without written permission. All other trademarks are the property of their respective owners. John Wiley & Sons, Inc. is not associated with any product or vendor mentioned in this book.

Cover design by Wiley
Cover image: © ml1413/Getty Images
Inside cover background: © Vidio/stock.adobe.com

Set in 11.5/14.5 pts and BerkeleyStd by Straive, Chennai, India.

For anyone who has ever, or will ever, become a carer for someone they love.
And, for Dad.

Contents

Introduction:
Ducks on drugs

'I need you,' Dad's panicked voice comes through the phone.

'What's going on, Dad?' I respond, knowing he is in a hospice surrounded by medical professionals, so it's unlikely to be an emergency—or at least not one that can't be managed swiftly by the skilled team *in the building* from which he is calling.

'I just can't work it out, what to do next,' he continues. 'I feel so anxious. Can you come?' he pleads, sounding younger than his 68 years but with a fearful tone I am getting more used to.

'Of course, Dad, I'm on my way. See you soon.'

I tell my saint of a husband and two small children, aged three and six, that while I have been gone all day and just walked in the door, I now have to turn around and head back to the hospice. My eldest sobs. She doesn't understand why the person she's been patiently waiting for all day is going to miss yet another bedtime.

'It's not forever, my love, it's just for now. Papa needs me,' I explain, blinking back tears and feeling literally torn between the two places I need to be. I grab some fresh clothes, kiss my husband and bribe my children with chocolate, which will no doubt make the impending bedtime harder but is necessary to get out the door. On the way I field a call from a family member overseas, who I gently encourage to come home if they want to spend any time with Dad while he is still alive. I imagine grappling heavily with the weight of that decision, they direct their angst directly back at me; a spray of verbal venom not intended for me but with nowhere else to go in that moment. I understand — living on the other side of the world when someone you love is dying would be awful. By the time they are done, I am drenched in their discomfort but my body is on autopilot: turning off the car, grabbing my overnight bag, pressing the lock button on my keys and walking through the electric doors to find Dad at the entrance of the hospice, waiting impatiently for me.

I cut the call short, take a deep breath and put my half-smile on. Not an inappropriately smiley smile — that would be too much for a place where people go to die. Just enough to momentarily pacify my panicked dad. It appears to have the desired effect, his shoulders dropping visibly when he sees me. We go back to his room, troubleshoot his confusion around why his medications don't seem to be doing their job of saving his life, call the doctors in, send them out. Then, we walk. Walking is probably a stretch — shuffling is more apt. We shuffle for hours around the hospice grounds, car parks and nearby garden. Dad's feet no longer fit in shoes nor slippers, so he shifts his giant bare feet forward one by one, swollen with fluid that signal his body's systems are starting to shut down. He doesn't say so, but I am certain he thinks that if we just keep moving we'll out-shuffle what we both know is coming.

I walk slowly beside him, hand in hand. Talking. Listening. Breathing. Externally I'm there, but internally I'm wading through the layers of complexity, responsibility and others' emotions (let alone my own, which there is no time for) that in quiet moments make me feel like I am a suitcase that has been stuffed too full and is about to erupt like a volcano of socks and undies. Between young children, a dying dad, a family tree that is far from straightforward, a career/need to contribute income and maintaining some semblance of relationships, I am as under the pump as a person can get. I'm well under. Like core-of-the-Earth under.

We finally return to the hospice and communicate to the nurse on duty that there's been some distress we can't quite manage. Speaking in code but I think referring to getting the delicate and temperamental balance of the medical, physical and emotional needs of a dying person just right, she says we need to get our ducks in a row. And no offence to her or to ducks, but ours are running around in circles and bumping into each other. There's a strong chance our ducks are on drugs, and I couldn't get them in a row if I tried.

These experiences, and hundreds more just like them, were the catalyst for this book.

Becoming Next of Kin

I have always loved writing (and speaking) about hard things. I've made a career out of sharing things people don't tend to talk about in the hope those experiencing them will feel less alone—the sort of light-in-the-dark stuff that's less taboo now but that I always needed and couldn't find when I was going through my own hard things. So, when I knew I was losing Dad, I started writing about it. Early in the piece, while my thoughts and ideas were still muddy, I tapped 'unimaginable loss' into my keyboard before quickly deleting it. Losing Dad wasn't unimaginable. It was very imaginable. So imaginable, in fact, that every single one of us will go through it. And yet, no one seemed to be talking about it.

It makes sense that we don't want to imagine what losing them might feel like, or what living without them might be like. Losing people we love hurts. So why write a book about it? Well, this statistic will shock you, but 100 per cent of the people you know and love are going to die. None of us are getting out of here alive. But while preparing for someone's death is a core theme in this book, my sincere hope is that in reading it you learn something about life. After all, death is the most powerful filter we have. You mightn't be caring for or losing someone you love in this moment, but the truth is that you will. And when that time comes, my intention is to give you a guide, a light on the path to illuminate the darkness and keep you company.

Because caring for someone you love is hard enough without having to navigate our complicated health, aged and death care systems without a map, compass or even a bottle of water. We're already thirsty, and we're about to get thirstier.

As our society ages and demographics change, we live with more chronic disease and what doctors call co- and multi-morbidities, meaning living with multiple conditions at the same time. It's a decent trade-off: more time to get sick is the price we pay for longevity. But we also have a healthcare system under increasing pressure, and—if we're honest—one that doesn't truly *value* care. You only need to look at the way we reward nurses, aged care and childcare workers to see that. But what about the people who don't choose care as a profession and yet find themselves in the position of caring for someone they love? In Australia, the Australian Bureau of Statistics reported there were three million carers in 2022—around one in eight people. In the same year, an Infometrics report revealed that one in seven people in New Zealand are unpaid carers, and that's supposedly wildly underestimated. Similar reports from the UK and the US suggested it was around one in five in both countries at that time.

However, it's hard to compare because Australian figures don't always count many people who may not fit the carer criteria but are still caring for someone with a:

- Terminal illness
- Chronic/complex health condition
- Mental illness
- Addiction or substance use disorder
- Significant neurodiversity.

Or even just people caring for small children. If they did, I suspect our carer numbers would be much higher.

Perhaps, like me, you're part of what's known as the sandwich generation—trying to care for young children and ageing parents at the same time. Can we just scratch that term? A sandwich sounds great: hello, fluffy bread, delicious fillings and lashings of condiments. However, caring for two groups of people with entirely different needs, at the same time, is far from a picnic. Sure, it's a sandwich . . . if the bread had teeth, was toasted in a fiery pit of hell and then dropped on the floor. Okay, that might be a bit dramatic. But my point is that even vicious sandwiches are easier to eat when you have some tools with which to eat them. This book contains some of those tools.

While these chapters hang on my experience of caring for someone with a terminal illness, care shares common ground no matter the context. Fuelled entirely by love and caffeine, carers wade alone through the murky, confusing and at times heartbreaking systems designed (and trying desperately) to support us. When we fall pregnant, there are millions of books, podcasts, articles and social media accounts to show us how to navigate every waking, breathing, crying moment of growing a child and raising one. But when it comes to walking someone through what happens when the life they're already living goes awry (or comes to its inevitable end), there's very, very little to show us the way. This book contains mine and Dad's stories, but they are stories in which anyone can find themselves. They are informed by science and infused, where appropriate, with expert opinion. Everyone is welcome here, because while the experience of care is universal (albeit more and more outsourced), we feel so very alone when we're in it. I hope what you read here will assure you that you are actually far from alone. There are Next of Kin all around you, walking the same path with their people. This book is about bringing us together and reminding us of why we're here in the first place.

If we take a giant step back, our purpose in life isn't to get bigger mortgages and more followers, it's to love and care for one another. Care is intertwined with our humanity, our most basic need to survive. While our modern lives may at times seem inherently self-serving, we are tribal—designed to be here for each other. Ancient philosophies have long preached our interconnectedness. It's primal. As old as time. And while care is purposeful, meaningful work, it's inherently undervalued. Carers are mostly unpaid, largely women (no surprises there) and often people still in the workforce because they need to earn a living while trying to care for someone they love who is likely going through the hardest time of their life. In short, the system is set up to fail. How many other global systems do you know that operate on—and are powered by—love? To give you some context, in 2021, global spending on health reached a staggering $9.8 trillion, accounting for 10.3 per cent of global gross domestic product. But unpaid care, if compensated, would cost us another $11 trillion—and that's at minimum wage. The World Economic Forum says that in 2035, the care economy will be worth at least six times the value of the space economy.

The care economy is at the heart of our survival and our progress, because it's the thing that sustains human activity not just for now, but for the future. We need to champion carers, reform policy to better support them and rewrite the narrative around care. In the meantime, we have no choice but to empower ourselves and our Next of Kin to become better advocates. What I know is that individuals and families are very capable if they have some guidance. They don't need to be rescued; they just need to learn how to drive the boat.

Next of Kin are driven and impassioned stakeholders, because we're often watching on, feeling helpless, as someone we love suffers. Helplessness is to motivation as gasoline is to fire. Don't get me wrong, when our health hits the fan, we certainly want medical professionals to be holding the scalpel, writing the script and making the diagnoses. But it's our people we want around us—advocating for our wishes and ensuring we're getting the best care available while we focus on healing or just surviving. With evidence-based medical information now at our fingertips (thanks internet), we hold the keys to better care and improved outcomes as true partners in any healthcare journey. Taking advantage of the knowledge available to us can translate to more time with the people we love most, and we get there by starting to think more critically about our care.

What to expect from this book

What you'll find here is by no means a definitive guide, and I am by no means a doctor, a psychologist or even particularly good at life admin.

What I have done is spent two-and-a-half years getting the very best care education one can get by being the primary carer and advocate for my dad, on top of a 20-year career gathering advice from leading experts and communicating health information to the public. But care, grief and loss don't fit into a simple-to-follow framework you'd see on breakfast TV, a TikTok video or even in a whole book. These experiences aren't neat. They're messy—like commercial-grade messy.

While care is universal, the details are unique. That said, there are some common domains to care, and they form the four parts of this book:

- **Medical care:** Navigating the system, receiving a diagnosis, understanding treatment options and advocating for someone you love.
- **Physical care:** Caring for your person and yourself (whether it's a marathon or a sprint), working with your care team, finding coping strategies and life on the frontline.
- **Legal and financial care:** Having difficult conversations, planning ahead to avoid legal headaches and dealing with the costs of care—of which there are many.
- **Emotional care:** Making memories, death, dying and grief, celebrating life through ceremony and finding meaning.

What you'll find in these pages is everything I wish I'd had when I started my care journey. While there's no 'framework', I've included some subheadings, lists and even dot points, all drenched in humanity. I wish this book (ANY book) could help us 'hack' the most challenging and transformative human experience that is caring for someone we love, but this one can't and none I've come across yet will. My hope is that instead it will hold your hand and act as *your* Next of Kin. Solid, dependable and a good time ... even in the worst of times.

I could've written a book's worth of content on every chapter here, not because I'm an expert in any of them but because there's just so much to it—care is nuanced, complicated and very, very personal. However, my intention is to give you just enough on any topic to point you in the right direction, but not so much you feel overwhelmed—the internet will do a good enough job of that for you. Think of this as your textbook—mark it up, fold the pages, go wild with highlighter. And, while not everyone loves talking about hard things, this book has been designed to bring to the table. Let it start big conversations while everyone is still present to have them. Over tea and cake is best.

Confession: Even with my high levels of health literacy and emotional intelligence (most of the time), I have some fairly intense fears around ill health, and particularly death. I have always been a worst-case-scenario thinker, and it doesn't take much for me to start planning my own funeral. Headache? Brain tumour. Knee pain? Bone cancer. Can't find my keys? Dementia. I don't know how to get around that. Fear is a powerful force—I'm terrified of my life being cut short and leaving my children without their mother. Which is why I hold so much compassion for anyone going through any kind of healthcare journey, particularly one with a poor prognosis. I tell you this here to acknowledge how hard it is to put some of the ideas in this book into practice—and so you know that whether I'm speaking to your person or to you directly, I am always also speaking to myself. We're all in this together.

If you are a carer, this book is for you. It will help you better care for the people around you. If you are a patient, this book is for you. It will help you better understand how to get the most out of the people around you. If you are a healthcare professional, this book will help you better support yourself and your patients—who are lucky to have you.

I'm grateful to be here with you, honoured by your trust and hope you reach for this book (and share it around) whenever life calls for it.

—Casey

P.S: One thing I know is this: carers need support. At the back of this book you'll find an invitation to join the Next of Kin community, where you'll find like-minded people, resources and education. I'd highly recommend you come and join us whenever you feel ready. Also, we have snacks.

P.P.S: It goes without saying that nothing in here is a substitute for medical, legal, financial or spiritual advice. Your situation will be different to mine, and you must ensure you are advised appropriately by people who know what they are talking about. You can check out the Resources section at the end of the book if you want to dig deeper.

P.P.P.S: It would be remiss of me to not acknowledge my privilege here. I am an able-bodied, moderately sane and healthy white woman in one of the richest countries on Earth. When Dad got sick, I was in a position to move my family across the country to care for him. We were able to survive on one income when I needed to dial work right back so I could be with Dad, and we have a raft of beautiful family and friends who acted as glue and kept my little family alive while I was trying to do the same for Dad. It's not lost on me how lucky I am, and that not everyone is in the same boat. If that's you, I hope this book makes your life a tiny bit easier.

P.P.P.P.S (last one I promise, I'm out of Ps): Because Dad is no longer with us, he's not here to review or approve this manuscript. In the beginning of his illness Dad was very private, sharing health details and his inner thoughts only with me and a small number of others. But Dad was a deep thinker, and we spent a lot of time analysing our (more importantly his) experience and talking about how we — as a society — could do care better. It's those thoughts and ideas that form a large part of this book's bones.

What I can share with you is that he trusted me and my writing implicitly and was always in favour of raw truth and generosity of spirit, both of which you'll find in this book. Luckily, I started writing while Dad was still here and I was able to interview him a number of times to gather some words directly from the source and get the patient's perspective, which in my opinion is the most important one. So Dad is infused in these pages, and I'm delighted to get to share some of his greatness with you. And when I say he was great, he was truly the greatest. Even though this book only captures the period of his illness (as well as the aftermath), I'm mindful that he had lived a full 66 years before his life was upended by disease. So, I hope his greatness shines through to you, even when the subject material doesn't allow him to be his greatest self.

Before I do share some of that greatness with you, please know this. Dad and I aren't ones for small talk. You'd be more likely to find us in the corner of the party going deep than you would getting us to ask a stranger, 'So, ah … Sandra. What do you do?' In the following pages, we're inviting you to our corner of the party. In it we may cry, we'll definitely laugh and at some point we'll probably dance. You're in for the ride of Dad's lifetime.

PART I

Medical Care

Navigating the system, receiving a diagnosis, understanding treatment options and advocating for someone you love.

CHAPTER 1

Pull the rug

You never forget where you are when you receive one of *those* calls. We spend our lives trying desperately to avoid them, but they are simply the price of being alive and loving other alive people. I was in an entirely unfamiliar holiday rental 4000 kilometres away from Dad when I received his call, but I can explain in detail the room in which I stood, sat and then slumped as I felt the blood drain from the top of my head to my toes while he delivered his news.

It was the first week of June in 2021, and I was riding high on a wave of media coverage, positive reviews and celebrity endorsements for my first book. And yet, unbeknownst to me, on the very same day my book was released, my dad was admitted to a hospital in Perth, the isolated but magical city I'd grown up in but had left some 15 years prior to carve out a media career and begin a serious love affair with the harbour city of Sydney.

My husband and I, as well as our two small children, had travelled to Wagga Wagga, a regional town a five-hour drive from our home in Sydney, to celebrate my husband's graduation from his master's degree. After three years of studying every weekend (and many hours on the tools myself either solo parenting or editing his assignments), I forced him into a gown and cap and gathered the family to celebrate. It was a happy day, a proud day, and one that would end in despair.

Dad had texted the day before to ask if we could have a quick chat soon, and—blissfully unaware of his plight—I had arranged to call him after the graduation, as always asking if he was okay before signing off. In retrospect he didn't really answer me, but he responded cheerily enough that it didn't ring any alarm bells. He was clever like that. I'm a firm believer anyone who can survive longer than two minutes after receiving a 'can we talk' message without speed-dialling the source deserves a medal. I am not that person. Yet, wanting to give my husband his rare moment in the sun, I allowed myself to remain caught up in what was in front of me, missing Dad's ninja-like avoidance of answering whether everything was, in fact, okay.

Which, when we connected later that evening, I would find out it was not.

Him: 'Sweetheart, I have some bad news.'

Me: 'About what?'

Him: 'About my health.'

Me: 'What's going on?'

Him: 'I have mesothelioma.'

Me, panicking and prematurely firing off a poor guess: 'Blood cancer?'

Him: 'It's cancer of the pleura—the lining of the lung...'

Dad's voice faded out and I felt hot and prickly, like I'd stepped outside of my body. I tried to orient myself in space and time by snapping into action, putting him on speakerphone so I could quickly google what we were talking about, and more importantly what sort of prognosis he was looking at. He slowly walked me through the details as I asked a million questions and tried to maintain some level of decorum, my eyes frantically jumping from link to link.

Fatal. Incurable. Six months. Eight months. Twelve months.

No doubt mustering every inch of courage he had and already looking for the silver lining, Dad insisted he felt 'wide awake' and 'blessed' for the wake-up call. And me? I cried all night, knowing deep in my bones that, sooner rather than later, I was going to lose my beloved dad.

If I think back to my childhood, I've always had an unquenchable thirst for a few things. The first is two-minute noodles. Even though they contain the nutritional equivalent of sand, I still love them and would eat them every day if I could get away with it and still be taken seriously as an adult. The second is pop song lyrics. I can't remember most people's names or my logins to pretty much anything, but I can remember every word to a wide array of 1990s R&B songs (which comes in less handy than you'd think). But the third is a thirst for knowledge, and it was always medicine and people that most piqued my interest. I probably should have been a doctor, but I was too busy studying the art of being a delinquent at high school to get the grades for medicine. Instead, I built a career out of asking doctors questions, and I think my hunger for answers was evident in me from when I was very, very little.

In 1988, Dad had a friend come out from the UK to stay with us. This wasn't uncommon—our house was a revolving door of Dad's friends, girlfriends and not-quite-girlfriends, as well as people brought in to help cover the rent. She was doing her PhD in something to do with the role of group therapy in adult education. One of the groups she observed and tested was men with HIV, which was—in the 1980s—pretty much a death sentence. She brought groups into our home so they could connect and talk about their illnesses and lives, and so she could watch what occurred.

This is an extract from her thesis:

The various members of the household, including Jack's four-year-old child Casey, moved in and out of whichever workshop was taking place with little apparent discomfort, listening, joining in the questioning and moving out again when a more pressing engagement beckoned. During the Body Positive

workshop, Casey set up a miniature shop in her bedroom, and cajoled individuals into leaving the group in order to engage in trading according to her rules. At other times she joined in any group which took her fancy, taking readily to the turn-taking with questions, and occasionally pulling a question in her direction by sighing loudly and remarking to no one in particular that 'I haven't had a turn in ages'.

This curiosity has remained with me my whole life. I vaguely remember those workshops; the memories must be stored in the same mental cabinet as the lyrics of the hot hits of the '90s. In subsequent conversations, I've learned my 'cajoling' of the participants basically meant taking them by the hand and pulling on their arm until they had no choice but to come with me. Bearing in mind this took place at a time when people thought you could transmit HIV by shaking hands or even touching the same surface, and people with the virus were largely shunned due to fear of transmission, I feel proud and grateful that I lived in a home where that sort of experience was available to me. Thinking about four-year-old me sitting in a circle with grown, sick men, asking questions and trying to be part of the conversation to understand the illness and the people living with it, feels like a very accurate representation of what I'd grow up to be. I'm fascinated by both clinical care and communication, and how knowledge and action truly are power when it comes to our health. This obsession served me well when Dad—and I, by proxy—were thrown into the fraught and fragmented medical system.

At that stage in my life, I'd spent 15 or so years reporting on, producing content for and facilitating conversations with key players in healthcare—a system I thought I knew intimately. Turns out the system and I were about to go from casual hook-ups to a shotgun wedding, for better or worse, in (mainly) sickness and (less so) health. My experience would give me a front-row seat to just how complex and challenging the system is to navigate, even with my high level of health literacy, communication experience and handy contacts.

I'd find myself scratching my head and imagining how much harder it would be if English wasn't your first language, you didn't have a family support network, or you couldn't read or write. This lit my desire to help others better navigate the system, so to orient you I'm going to start by sharing a bird's-eye, macro view—a YOU ARE HERE mark. If knowledge is power, then having a solid grip of the basics to work from is like taking the plug and sticking it into the electrical socket. It's step one of many, but every journey begins with the first step.

The care landscape

Australia is widely known to have one of the best healthcare systems in the world. It's not high-tax, high-return, topping-the-happiest-places-to-live-lists Scandinavia, but it's pretty good. It's by no means perfect, but show me a healthcare system—any system supporting a nation—that is. Unlike the US, where you pay or you suffer (making insurance benefits the holy grail of employment), Australia's healthcare system offers a two-pronged approach to medical care. Much like the UK's NHS, we have a public scheme called Medicare available to all, and a private system available to those willing—or able—to pay for it. An easy way to think about it is like when you travel with an airline. The public system could be thought of as economy and the private system is business class. It's an imperfect analogy because business class is considered better than economy, but the care you receive in the private system isn't necessarily better than what you'd receive in the public system—you just have more choice, shorter wait times and possibly a nicer seat.

Our public scheme, Medicare, is paid for by the federal and state governments (and therefore, by taxpayers). If you're an Australian citizen, permanent resident or applicable visa-holder, you can access free healthcare at bulk-billed medical clinics and public hospitals. Bulk-billing is where practitioners are paid directly by the government, so there's no out-of-pocket cost to the patient. The upside is that it doesn't cost anything; the downside is that unless it's an emergency, you're likely to have to wait (sometimes years) for specialist care and you'll have little to no say in who delivers it. You might be able to choose your general practitioner (GP) but if you need more complex care, you'll get whatever surgeon or specialist can pick up your case — whenever they can get to it.

Our private system is paid for by industry (insurers) and individuals — people who choose to either pay for care directly to the providers, or to health insurers in return for coverage, and then any gap between what insurers will pay and what medical professionals choose to charge. The government pays too by covering some of the costs of care and providing a private health insurance rebate to policy holders (to help offset the cost), as well as paying for public hospitals in which private patients can still receive care. People who choose not to take out private health insurance are slogged with what's called the Medicare levy surcharge, designed to encourage us to take out private health insurance and take the pressure off the public system. The upside of the private system is that you have more control over who treats you, and in theory you shouldn't have to wait as long for care. The downside is that you'll pay fairly handsomely for the care you receive — whether that's paying for insurance or the price of treatment (or, more likely, both).

There are adjacent systems, services and schemes you may have to work with on the journey too, such as welfare (Centrelink), aged care (My Aged Care) and disability (the National Disability Insurance Scheme). These work alongside our healthcare system to deliver care (see figure 1.1).

Within the healthcare system, there are various subsystems, including:

- **Primary care:** This is usually what we call general practice — your first port of call when you're not well and the subsystem you'll likely interact with most. Primary care is the backbone of our healthcare system and arguably the subsystem under the most pressure.

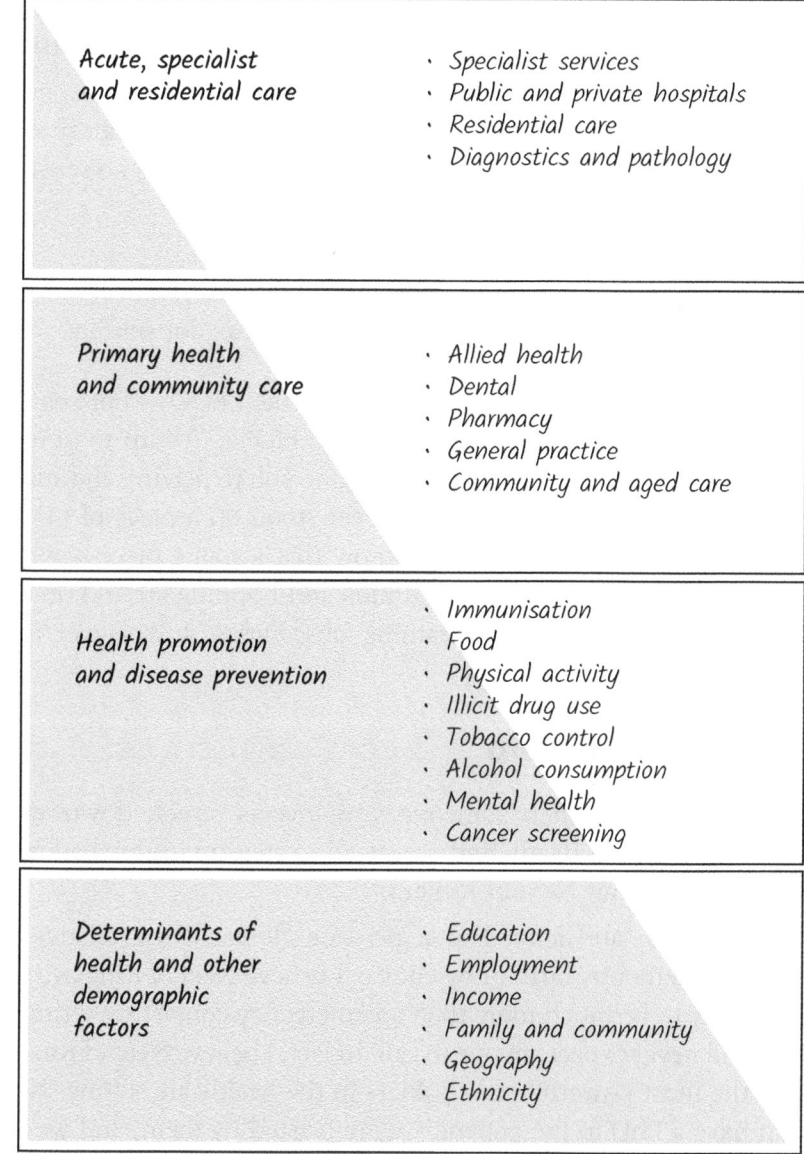

Figure 1.1 The layers of the Australian healthcare system

- **Secondary care:** The specialists we are referred to when primary care isn't enough—think cardiologists for our hearts, psychiatrists for our minds and orthopaedic surgeons for our bones.
- **Tertiary care:** The hospitals we go to when we need surgical or medical intervention (and little cups of jelly that make no sense nutritionally nor to anyone post-1994).
- **Allied health:** All the healthcare professionals who work alongside and support doctors and patients. Think physiotherapists, psychologists and pharmacists, for starters.

The subsystems are designed to fit together like LEGO—but *you* are the one playing with the colourful plastic blocks. It's up to you to come up with a design based on what game you're playing and make the pieces fit together. And if you've ever stood on a piece of LEGO in bare feet (hello, parents), you'll know that a rogue piece—while tiny—can cause all sorts of pain, drama and hopping around on the other foot while internally screaming obscenities at whatever tiny terrorist left it there.

In your Next of Kin era

So, what happens when someone you love is struck down with disease, disability or death, and you need to step up to the plate and play? You enter your Next of Kin era.

Next of Kin are defined as a person's closest living relative or relatives. Whether by birth or by choice, I believe Next of Kin have the opportunity to be much more than an emergency contact we write on a form and never expect anyone to call. In fact, I believe Next of Kin are one of the most powerful stakeholders in the healthcare setting. Next of Kin have a PhD in the patient; we are trusted by them, and we are one step removed from their experience. It's not happening *to* us, but in front of us. So, if there's anyone best positioned to provide support, it's Next of Kin. In the throes of illness, disability or mortality—whatever the patient is facing—their focus should be on the challenge in front of them. For that very reason and myriad others, it's hard for patients to be their own advocates. In the same way lawyers handle divorces and real estate agents sell houses, sometimes we need an intermediary to think strategically on our behalf. And care is no exception.

So, let's talk tactics. Pretend you're in the army for a moment. I have about as much experience in the military as I do in the Ferris wheel industry (and I may or may not have streamed too many action series), but bear with me. In any mission, there's usually a couple of main characters: a target or asset (which in our analogy is the patient), and a captain (which in this case is you). Working with and around you are other special ops teams and services, but the captain is the one assessing all the inbound intel, reading between the lines, advocating for what the asset wants or needs, and helping devise a strategy that supports not just the management of the illness or injury, but the person who has it.

I'm going to level with you—being the captain can be about as much fun as doing your tax return while cleaning out your gutters. My nickname in our family while caring for Dad was Drill Sergeant Casey. While my ego bristled when I learned of my new moniker (because we all like being liked), in the end I responded with: 'Damn straight, and it's Captain Drill Sergeant Casey to you.'

Unfortunately, someone has to be in charge when someone else's health, happiness and, in some circumstances, life, is on the line. In an ideal world some helpful fairy godmother would assemble a team around you, brief you (like in the movies) and then give you some kind of lanyard, whistle or at least an official-looking hat. But in this world, the real world, you're going to have to assemble that team—and run it—yourself.

It's not what you know...

Bearing in mind the required team will look different depending on your situation, here are a few key players that were vital in ours and who you might find helpful to have in your corner.

- **A (great) GP.** Good GPs are worth their weight in whatever is the next level up from gold. Ideally, you'll have a relationship with them already so they'll understand your history, but if you don't then you can build one. You might have to kiss a few frogs, but keep trying until you find the right fit. They'll be able to distil results to you if specialists prove hard to understand (or get an appointment with), and they can help escalate things if you aren't getting what you need. In short, they can crack proverbial skulls if needed.

- **Someone to support your person's mental health.** This could be a psychologist, counsellor or spiritual advisor. Having someone they can unpack things with that *isn't* you is vital for them, because there will be things they don't want to share with you, or anyone else they know—especially if they are facing their mortality.

- **Someone to support your mental health.** This could be any of those listed above but it could also be a skilled and trusted friend who knows when their level of support is no longer sufficient and you need professional support. Having someone who is trained and paid to support you is advantageous if you can afford it. Some hospitals, hospices and support services (such as Cancer Council Australia) have free counselling services and are worth exploring.

- **Someone who speaks fluent 'medicine'.** Got a friend who's a doctor or nurse? A second cousin who's a pharmacist? Get yourself someone who can decode for you beyond the guidance this book and Dr Google can provide. They can be invaluable at translating if they're willing to give you some of their time, and you'll struggle to get around if you don't speak the language.

My advice? Work hard on building solid relationships with all these people. You want them to like you so they'll be more likely to go above and beyond for you, and therefore for the person you're caring for. And if you find the right people, you'll learn fast that the old adage is true: it's not what you know, but who.

Hindsight

In our last interview, I asked Dad if there was something he wished he'd known earlier in the journey.

'I wish I'd known that the medical system is not well suited to managing complex diseases like this,' he told me. 'I've met some wonderful people but I think our health system has a long way to go in terms of really managing individuals well throughout the process from go to whoa, and leaves a lot to be desired in so many ways. I'm very lucky that I have a brain and some great advocacy and people I can turn to for advice when I'm stuck, and I really feel for people who don't have those things.'

If that's you, you're in luck. This book has been designed to hold your hand, sit with you while you have a cuppa and be a resource for you to turn to when you need guidance.

Setting an intention

Oh dear. 'Setting an intention' makes me sound like a meditation teacher. For the record, I'm not; and if I'm honest with you I can't bloody stand meditation. But I do think that when it comes to care (because it's often such a long and winding road), having a set of words to live by is smart. They'll become an anchor when seas get stormy, and the forecast shows a 100 per cent chance of wild weather.

My words came about while sitting in a café with one of my mentors. I lean on people when they've got direct experience with whatever I'm going through, and I'm always richer for their wisdom. I was speaking passionately (read: bitching) about Dad, for whom I had just moved my family across the country, from Sydney back to my hometown of Perth, so I could care for him in his time of need. Dad, grappling with his own grief around his diagnosis, as well as all the other challenges that come with being an adult, was being (and I say this with compassion) a pain-in-the-ass. The same flawed, perfectly imperfect pain-in-the-ass he'd always been, but now with the added complexity of a terminal medical diagnosis. And he was, understandably, not handling it well.

Let me clarify here that I've obviously never been in his shoes, and I held (still hold) so much compassion for his situation. He was living anyone's worst nightmare in having to say goodbye to the people he loves most, sooner than he'd have liked to. So, there's zero judgement, just the experience of being on the receiving end of some of his discomfort—which is putting it mildly. Carers are usually compassionate, empathic people. They care, so they care. And as the closest person to the patient, they usually cop whatever mood, emotion or feeling the person in the hot seat is experiencing. Learning to protect yourself while supporting them is imperative to ensuring that you—as the carer—aren't left with too much residual scar tissue.

But back to the café. I was conveying to my mentor friend that I was a male bee's genitals away from putting us back on a plane—ready to tell Dad he could care for himself if this was how he was going to behave. That sounds callous, and I was no doubt talking a big game I wouldn't have ever followed through on, but it's a good example of how a Next of Kin relationship can be tested during these times, no matter how good and strong a foundation the relationship has.

'But you won't walk away,' she said, gently steering me back to the land of the rational. 'Because on the other side of this experience, when you're packing it away in yourself, you'll know you did absolutely everything you could to make this awful time a tiny bit better for him. You'll regret nothing, and it'll make living with the loss easier.'

These words became my North Star, the ones I said to myself frequently and professed to others when they were grappling with their own role in walking Dad home. They saved me numerous times because they reminded me this wasn't forever, and there *was* something on the other side of this. When I read those words back they make me feel as guilty now as I did thinking them then, because between me and Dad, only one of us was able to say them. My inner world went to war with itself frequently—how could I look forward to the future when it was a future Dad wouldn't have? It's not that I couldn't live without him—I'd been through enough hard things to know I could, even though I really didn't want to—but looking forward felt like I was being disloyal to his experience.

The truth is, if you're going to dedicate your time to caring for someone else, you have to have something that is reserved only for you. Even if it's just a few words. They'll be your lifeline when you feel like you're drowning—and you will feel like you're drowning, no matter how strong a swimmer you think you are. You will find yourself well and truly outside of the flags, being sucked out to sea by rips and wishing you'd paid more attention to that CPR class you took once. This is the reality of trying desperately to save someone you love, while making sure you don't drown in the process.

CHAPTER 2

This is going to hurt

Dad's lifetime relationship with fitness had been patchy at best, and in an attempt to get fit at the ripe age of 66, he decided to hit the local pool to swim laps. He was one of those annoying people who always had an athletic build regardless of how little actual athletics he did, and while he had been a decent swimmer in the past, that day he was just looking to blow out the cobwebs and turn his arms over. Halfway through his first lap he was struggling, and by the time he touched the tiles at the other end, he was gasping for breath. Knowing this was beyond a lack of sheer cardiovascular grunt, he went to his general practitioner (GP), who ordered a scan of his lungs to see what was going on.

'Have you ever come into contact with asbestos?' the radiographer asked.

Dad's stomach dropped. Such a specific question about such a toxic substance couldn't be good.

'Ah, yes—many years ago...' he trailed off, already knowing his response wasn't going to elicit any sort of diagnostic clarity from the person taking the pictures, and that he'd instead need to undergo the torturous wait for another doctor's appointment to get the results. I'm not clear on exactly what happened next—I was still in blissful ignorance on the other side of the country, and Dad was strategically keeping me in the dark until he knew what he was dealing with. His suspicion there was indeed something wrong deepened when he was admitted to hospital to drain six litres of fluid off his left lung, which had been covertly accumulating for some time. Testing of the fluid confirmed a diagnosis of mesothelioma—an aggressive and deadly cancer that occurs in the thin layer of tissue (mesothelium) around internal organs, most commonly in the pleura (the lining of the lungs), as was the case for Dad.

You may have already worked this out based on the radiographer's pointed question, but mesothelioma is caused by exposure to asbestos, a fibrous mineral substance found naturally that was known as a miracle mineral. Durable, cheap and accessible, it is fireproof, soundproof and so versatile that at one point it could be found in more than 3000 home and building products. Its use accelerated in a post-war housing boom from the late 1940s, well into the 1970s and beyond, before we learned it was a carcinogen and started phasing it out in the 1980s. Banning it altogether is recent history in Australia—it was still mined here until 1984 and not actually banned from use until 2003. Until then, Australia was one of the highest users of asbestos in the world and Western Australia was home to our most prolific asbestos mine, which I've since heard described as Australia's biggest industrial disaster. Asbestos is still present in one in three homes across the country, and thanks to the popularity of home renovation shows on TV we're now seeing another wave of exposure as people attempt DIY while unknowingly working with asbestos.

There's every chance you or someone you love doesn't have the rare cancer that is mesothelioma, a mouse compared to the lions that are, say, heart disease, dementia or other cancers (such as lung or bowel cancer) in terms of lives taken each year. While it's not common, mesothelioma provides a good thought experiment here when it comes to disease. Awareness campaigns say of asbestos that 'one fibre kills', while—just like many risk factors when it comes to our health—science and probably common sense would argue that more exposure equals more risk. But it's not a rule; someone could have lots of exposure to asbestos and never end up with asbestos-related disease, and—without being alarmist—someone could have a one-off or minimal exposure and end up dying from it. But this catchcry exists because if you're unlucky enough to have one little fibre of asbestos enter your body and make a home there, it could be enough to—eventually—make you very sick. It can take a long time for exposure to asbestos to turn into a symptomatic disease: between 20 and 60 years. In Dad's case, it was 50. These tiny little fibres, planted 50 years ago, nestled in Dad's lungs, not making a peep until many, many years later when they would take his life.

From little things, big things grow: Why we get sick

One of the things that seems to happen when someone gets sick is some level of self-enquiry: why did this happen to me? Or, for their loved ones: why did this happen to them? Most of the time it's a fruitless game, and blame is unhelpful at best and damaging at worst—outside of a setting where there is some sort of legal negligence or liability. The energy spent working out why is perhaps better spent on figuring out a strategy to improve their outcomes. However, without taking you back to high school science, I think it's worth acknowledging the reasons we get sick.

With any illness or injury, three elements need to be present: a source (or trigger), a host and a reaction. In Dad's case, the source was the asbestos, Dad was the host and the reaction was mesothelioma. In a car accident, the accident (or car) is the source, the victim is the host and their injuries are the reaction. But the outcome may not always be the same. For example, someone could smoke their whole life and not end up with lung cancer, or two different people could be in the same car accident and not be injured in the same way.

Dad was simply unlucky, and bad luck is one reason we get sick or injured. But there are other common causes, including:

- **Our genetics.** Our genes play a significant role in our physical and mental health, though science often debates how much and for what conditions. Personalised medicine is banking on genetic testing being able to predict the future risk of disease, and shape both preventative measures and better, more effective treatments. It's the closest thing we have to a crystal ball; while it's not an exact science or a map, it is possibly a compass we can use as a guide.

- **Our environment.** The places we inhabit have a big impact on our health. From climate change and pollution to sick buildings, toxic workplaces, transmissible diseases from animals, dangerous environmental agents and obesogenic food systems, the world we live in—both global and local—can be a source of illness and injury. Unlike our genetics, our environment is a little more within our control and worth our attention.

- **Our lifestyle and behaviours.** If I had to choose a preferred source of illness or injury, this would be my favourite one. Why? Because it's the one most within our control. The big-ticket killers in most developed countries (and many developing ones too) are diseases of the:
  - Heart (such as cardiovascular diseases)
  - Body (such as cancers)
  - Brain (such as neurodegenerative diseases like Alzheimer's disease, as well as stroke)
  - Gut (such as type 2 diabetes and related metabolic diseases).

If you look at the risk factors for any of these diseases, they are largely the same. Things like:

- **Poor diet:** Not enough fresh fruits and vegetables and too many salty, fatty, sugary, processed foods (essentially, the fast-food-ification of our diet)
- **Not moving enough:** A sedentary lifestyle with little movement by way of deliberate or incidental exercise (AKA too much slouch and couch)
- **Excess body weight:** Being overweight or obese, usually as a result of both of the above (poor diet and a lack of exercise)

- **High blood pressure, cholesterol and blood sugars:** A trifecta of symptoms that may spell metabolic and therefore disease disaster
- **Unhealthy lifestyle choices:** Smoking (and now vaping) and/or drinking too much alcohol or taking illicit drugs.

Risk factors also tend to hunt in packs. For example, if you have high cholesterol, you're likely to have high blood pressure and be overweight or obese, and so on. The body doesn't just keep score, it plays dominoes. While most people enjoy a bag of chips or glass of wine and skip the gym here and there, our convenience climate of 24/7 access to anything we want has meant we need to move less than ever, especially when coupled with remote or flexible work arrangements and the blurred lines between work and home. Add in our increasingly stressful and busy lives, and it's easy for people to go into 'health debt'. Those tiny transactions stack up. As a result, most of us will die from a largely 'preventable' chronic disease that brings with it a period of illness before we go, and with that can come a level of helplessness that means we will eventually need to lean on someone we love.

To understand the origins of disease, medicine has for decades now worked on what it calls a biopsychosocial model. (Say it to your friends; it makes you sound really smart.) It basically means that there are **bio**logical or physical factors that contribute to disease, as well as **psycho**logical or mental factors and **social** factors — so, how connected we feel to our people, places and communities. But we don't just have to use this way of thinking to *determine* the causes of disease: we can also use it as a *model for wellbeing*, one that diverts us away from our biggest killers. So, throughout this book you'll find lessons intended to improve the biopsychosocial wellbeing of both you and your loved ones. (See? SMART.)

Winkless in Wagga

The night I received the news from Dad, I didn't sleep a wink. It hadn't even been two years since we lost my angel of a mother-in-law to brain cancer, and in that time I'd watched my own mother lose her partner of 27 years to oesophageal cancer, my high school best friend lose her life to addiction, mental illness and suicide, and my 17-year-old niece lose her hair and a large chunk of her high school experience to Hodgkin lymphoma. At the ripe age of 37 I'd long shed the childlike illusion that life is unicorns and rainbows, but if bad things came in threes … surely we were oversubscribed.

As the sun rose on a new but worse day, I took myself for a walk—partly to escape the house before my children woke and saw my puffy, sleepless eyes, and partly to give my racing thoughts somewhere to go. Dad and I were separated by a continent: me on the east coast of Australia and him on the west. My instinct said get on a plane, but reasoning said wait—panicking helped no one, and I didn't want to spook Dad by overreacting and rushing to his side. I needed external consultation, and there was only one person to call—an old boss turned dear friend who'd lived an eerily similar life to mine and lost her own father at around the same age.

'Drop everything and GO,' she told me after a teary exchange, empathically and intuitively knowing what my news meant and the hurt it would inevitably deliver.

'You'll never regret getting on a plane now, the rest will work itself out.'

I took her advice, and I'll be forever grateful I did. It's worth reminding you that this was June 2021, a time when masks were worn, arms were (or controversially weren't) jabbed, and much of the world couldn't come together to celebrate or commiserate. Many weren't allowed to leave their homes. Determined not to become one of the poor souls pleading with politicians via the *Today* show for a travel exemption (or heaven forbid, saying goodbye to Dad over FaceTime), I booked us flights and got my little family on a plane to Perth. We landed to a midday press conference with our then-premier announcing that at midnight, just 12 hours later, the border would be shut behind us indefinitely. Thanks universe.

A day later, we eagerly awaited the results of the airport COVID tests that would allow us to leave our accommodation and roam free. Finally cleared, we arranged to meet Dad at a local café, still open thanks to Western Australia's then almost-COVID-free status. I watched from inside the glass windows as he arrived, taking a moment to stop at the door and take off his glasses so he could wipe some tears away. My heart in my mouth, he walked toward me, looking just like him but maybe a little more drawn, and gave me the sort of hug you get very few of in a lifetime — one that says, 'I love you, I'm still here, and somehow everything is going to be okay.' Of course, this wasn't true. But never let the truth get in the way of a good hug.

Over the coming weeks, we walked, talked, laughed, cried, drank, ate and breathed our new reality. We went to endless doctor's appointments and started to piece together the beginnings of a plan, me providing the extra set of eyes and ears necessary for navigating our complex medical system. At first, we felt in good hands. We were in the mesothelioma capital of the world (thanks to being the home of that now-closed asbestos mine), so Dad was quickly ushered into the Western Australian public hospital system. Though I knew I couldn't save him, I was certain I could buy him extra time. I'd dedicate myself to being the best carer and advocate I could, in the way I'd done everything else in my life — with hustle, caffeine and the power of asking lots of dumb questions.

Hurry up and wait

I'm not sure who designed the system of test — wait — get results, but I've got a fair bit to say to them and wouldn't mind at least sending them a sternly worded email. It's the reality of science, but it's also a special type of torture to ask someone potentially facing their mortality to wait days, sometimes even weeks, to learn their fate. I can order purple penis party straws on the internet and have them on my doorstep within 24 hours (thanks Amazon) but when it comes to waiting for life-changing medical results, our technologies, systems and bandwidths to implement them still seem to be stuck in 1952.

Diagnostic tests account for a decent chunk of our healthcare spend. I don't envy the professionals who are constantly weighing the need for investigation (and associated cost) with probability of disease. If I were in charge I'd just test everyone for everything all the time, which would bring with it a raft of challenges and dig the budget into a deeper, darker hole. While bigger, better minds than mine are no doubt working on ways to speed things up when it comes to diagnosis, there are three key things I've learned along the way that may hold some value if you or someone you love are undergoing the torturous wait for results.

#1: You can't hack the system, but you can work better within it

If you've ever had a pregnancy scan (or seen one in the movies), you might be familiar with the imaging technician (the person doing the scan) calling out a heartbeat or cute little body part as they go. When it comes to illness and disease, though, there's a clear delineation of role and responsibility, meaning the imaging technicians' job is to take the pictures, not usually to report to you in the moment. There's a good reason for this: the images have to be interpreted by a doctor who specialises in imaging (called a radiologist) and then delivered to your treating doctor (usually your GP or specialist), who can assess their relevance in the bigger picture of your health as well as the urgency of any treatment required, and the onus is on them to appropriately convey the results to you.

As tempting as it might be, don't ask the imaging staff for results or even what they can see; they aren't allowed to tell you (unless they're checking for a broken bone or something, which may be different). Likewise, don't try to read the technician's expressions for clues. They are trained to focus on the job, so any furrowed brows or strange looks may just be a reflection of their day or their face. They are working with complex machines and trying to find clear pictures of body parts in what to anyone else looks like mud. As hard as it may be, focus on staying still and letting them do their job.

Then, depending on myriad factors (such as the type of test, the results and your relationship with your doctor), how you receive those results can follow a number of paths. Your doctor may ask you to make another appointment to get the results, they may call or text you, or they may do nothing and expect you to follow up. Don't assume anything, including the old adage 'no news is good news'. It's *your* job to get *your* results.

Let's say you get tests on a Monday and your doctor receives the results on the Friday. On the following Monday, they contact you to say they have the results and need to see you to go through them, but they don't have any appointments until the following week, meaning you have to wait another whole week to find out what's going on. This is exactly where Next of Kin can come into play for a better result.

For example, at your testing appointment, find out what the turnaround time is for results and pre-book an appointment with your doctor so you aren't waiting to get back in. If your doctor calls you in the meantime and you don't need the appointment, then great—you can cancel it so it's free for someone else. This can save you and your loved one days in the purgatory of the unknown, especially if either of you are feeling anxious about the news or the stakes are high.

#2: You can't skip the worry, but you can learn to manage it

Worry is one of those useful emotions that can spring us into action, but it can also make us feel unnecessarily anxious in the face of things we're not actually in control of. Broadly speaking, I think we can agree there are two types of worries:

- **Useful worries** we can do something about
- **Useless worries** that won't change the outcome, no matter how hard we fret.

You can probably tell where I'm going with this. Triaging your worries into these crude categories is a noble goal but almost impossible to do when the outcome may have big, life-changing implications. While the results are out of your control, there are a couple of things you do have some control over:

1. Doing what you can to smooth the path by thinking ahead, communicating well, and anticipating needs and obstructions (such as by pre-booking a doctor's appointment to get results)
2. Managing the worry within yourself.

Managing worry looks different for everyone, but some self-enquiry is a good place to start. Ask yourself: 'Will worrying about this change the outcome?' If the answer is no, in theory you should try your best to let it go. But when that's impossible, all you can do is:

- **Give the worry somewhere to go.** Book a session with a therapist, trusted friend or family member to talk it out. You can even write it down, just get it out of your head.
- **Practise positive (or at least neutral) self-talk.** Yes, it's possible the result might not be what you want, but you're not there yet. There'll be plenty of time to worry, strategise and act if your fears materialise. Give yourself the gift of not knowing before you know. And, what if the results *do* go your way? Stranger things have happened.
- **If you can't let it go, allocate some designated worry time.** Pick a timeframe in which you're allowed to worry, like for your entire shower or while you do the dishes or for the next 10 minutes. Worry away, let your mind go where it needs to and acknowledge what comes up, then bring it back into the present. When your mind starts to wander back to the land of worry (which is its way of protecting you from potential danger), thank it for looking out for you and bring your focus back to the present moment. Mindfulness is your best friend here, and it's called a practice for a reason. Bring it back, bring it back and bring it back again.

When it comes to helping manage worry in others, I wish I had a magic wand here. All you can do is encourage them to practise the same things you are. Don't make promises you can't keep; if there's a chance things won't be okay, don't cheerlead them with pompoms of potentially false hope. I don't subscribe to the notion that without hope you have nothing. I'm not saying to embody doom and gloom, but optimism may serve you better than hope, especially when someone is staring down the barrel of a poor diagnosis or prognosis. Optimism is supportive: that things will be okay (and you will be okay), regardless of the outcome. Your role as a supporter is not to be a beacon of hope, it's simply to hold the flashlight. Offering assurances that aren't yours to give isn't helpful, nor do I think it is kind. You cannot hope them well, as much as you'd like to. Instead, aim for optimism.

Don't shoo their fears away, if they're afraid—let them be afraid. Rather than saying, 'That's not going to happen,' try saying something like, 'And if that happens, we will deal with it—one day at a time.' Rather than saying, 'Don't say that,' try saying, 'I hear you, that must feel scary. What can we do to make you feel better right now?'

It may also help to have a clear understanding of what you're testing for and why. I'd ask questions like:

- Why are we doing the test?
- What are we looking for?
- What might that mean?

This isn't for everyone: some people like being on a need-to-know basis, while others feel more empowered when they have more information. You'll know what will work best for you and your person.

#3: Keep an open mind

Like life, healthcare is a bit of a jigsaw puzzle. Some pieces fit together easily, while others seem like they belong to different puzzles altogether or appear to have been lost to the carpet gods. Results help paint a picture, but it's a picture of a moment in time and there's room for both human and scientific error. This depends wildly on the context, but if you take one set of results to 10 different practitioners, you'll likely get a slightly or significantly different interpretation of them, which is why becoming a great advocate for yourself and the people you love is so important. Knowing what questions to ask is key here, and we'll dive more into that in Chapter 4.

'I have bad news' and other sucky conversations

Before I lost Dad, I asked him what advice he'd give others delivering bad news to people they love so that between us we could share insights from the perspectives of carer or receiver and patient or deliverer. They are in no way groundbreaking, but they're the things we could put our finger on that helped (or would've helped) at that point in time, for what they're worth.

Tips for the deliverer of bad news, from Dad's perspective

Before I told anyone (including Casey), I contacted a counsellor I had worked with previously who I knew had had a dance with death too, navigating prostate cancer. He confirmed three things I had kinda figured:

1. There is no sugar-coating this variety of sh*t—so be gentle but direct with the news. Don't beat around the bush.

2. You know your people best, but in my experience it's best to tell loved ones alone, separately from others. Let them have their own experience of their emotions and ask their own questions. This isn't right for everyone; older couples who tend to live in each other's pockets, for example, may derive comfort from not being alone while receiving bad news.

3. Be careful who and how many people you tell in the early days. There is a tendency for such news to bring out a ghoulish aspect of human nature, full of curiosity and questions they probably don't understand the implications of asking. Ghouls love peddling bad news too, so my counsellor's sage advice was to keep it close, especially in the early days, to conserve my energy for my own deep musings.

I am deeply indebted to him for these insights. Somehow the news, its detail and its severity flowed out into the world in a way that never became a burden to me. Quite the opposite.

Tips for the receiver of bad news, from Casey's perspective

1. Write everything down. As cortisol floods your body and your nervous system prepares for war, your memory will be impacted. You will be grateful for the notes later. I pulled mine up years later to write this because there's no way I could remember clearly something so emotionally charged. Once you've cottoned on to the fact that you are receiving bad news, it's okay to say, 'Do you mind if we pause for a moment so I can grab a pen and paper and write this down? I want to make sure I get the details.'

2. If you consult Dr Google, you'll be served more information than you want or need at this stage. Some will be valuable, informing questions to ask at upcoming appointments. Some will be useless—wrong, out of date and muddying the waters of fact with fiction. Some again will be plain ugly. Choose your sources carefully—you can find a list of good ones in the Resources section at the end of this book. Steer clear of chat rooms, Facebook and personal blogs—you can use them later once you have the vital facts and some evidence-based information under your belt. And if your Aunt Sheila's friend's cousin's dog cured their totally unrelated cancer with organic panda saliva enemas from randomcures.com—take that advice with a big pinch of salt.

3. Try not to make it about you. Delivering bad news is hard enough without the deliverer having to manage your reaction to it. It's okay to be emotional if that's what comes up—I'm not suggesting you try to be stoic and push it down—but don't make them console you when they're already carrying the burden of the news. Thank them for telling you, acknowledge how hard telling you must've been, and know that it's okay to go away, digest and circle

(continued)

back to respond properly later. Breathe and slow down, even if your heart feels like it wants to break free of your chest and make a run for it. The best thing you can do for them right now is to provide a safe space to share the diagnosis and the feelings that go along with it.

These three skills—scribe, researcher and sounding board—are vital and will be used frequently on your Next of Kin journey. Get good at them now so they become second nature.

I'm glad I took these three skills seriously, because even after many years of navigating the healthcare system professionally, I was about to receive a crash course in what it's like to actually *need* the healthcare system, and what I'd find would blow my mind.

CHAPTER 3

Getting better, getting worse

Dad and I are sitting in a hospital waiting room for what feels like days but is probably an hour. An hour is a long time when you're waiting to learn your fate. We watch patients coming in and out of consulting rooms, silently and futilely hunting their faces for clues as to what our future might hold. After a long wait and a short walk down the corridor of doom we sit opposite a world-leading professor in Dad's disease, filled with mainly dread and what oddly feels like excitement but is probably a tiny flicker of hope. Not hope he'll be cured—we know enough to know that's not possible—but hope they'll offer us a miraculous solution that might allow Dad to stay with us a little longer.

I know first-hand that when emotions are heightened, memory tends to suffer. So, as we start talking, I set my phone to voice record and place it on the table in front of me. 'Are you recording me?!' she barks upon noticing, startling me and giving our long-awaited, anxiety-inducing appointment an abrasive and unfortunate start. I stammer out that I am, but that I was just about to ask her permission. Internal me is screaming, *I do this for a living! I would never disrespect you! I am not an idiot!* But I can tell from her tone and body language she has already decided I am not just an idiot, but a rude one at that.

I am hot and prickly and mortified. I pray for spontaneous combustion or at least a small lightning strike but with no such luck am forced to remain in the room. I'd been a fairly well-respected health journalist for 15 years, and yet I had managed to not only look stupid but also undermine myself as Dad's advocate. In hindsight, my brain sees the appropriate steps more clearly: prepare the device, ask permission, *then* hit record. The only explanation I can give for the delay is that with my nervous system in full flight, I was incredibly anxious about what we were about to hear. And, as someone who asks questions for a living, I was waiting for the exact right moment to interject and ask, *Do you mind if I record this so I can listen back later? I'm worried I'll forget the details.*

Of course, the doctor didn't know any of this and probably thought I was an international spy. Still, her heavy-handed response rattled me, making me more quiet and less self-assured than I'd usually be, given I was armed with hours of research, pages of notes and dozens of questions. While I own the error, if her intention was to put me back in my box, she succeeded.

Sadly, this is not an uncommon experience for carers. For the record, in some jurisdictions in Australia you don't require consent to record your appointment with a doctor, nurse or other health professional if the recording is simply for your own use (as in, you're not going to upload it to Facebook). But while I blundered this one (and the doctor didn't handle it particularly well either), I would always ask up front for permission, just because it's the right thing to do and is conducive to a respectful patient–doctor relationship. And I truly believe that better relationships can equal better results.

Given we already had the diagnosis of fatal, incurable mesothelioma, the appointment focused on treatment options and the tools available to Dad to tackle this unlucky and cruel disease in the hope it might buy some time. The doctor, a senior consultant with many years of delivering bad news under her belt, worked gently and methodically through our options: chemotherapy, immunotherapy or, conveniently, a clinical trial she was spearheading that was testing whether combining chemotherapy and immunotherapy against chemotherapy alone could extend life for patients with mesothelioma, for which the prognosis is always poor. We were told Dad had a 50 per cent chance of making it to a year, and that active treatment was his best chance of getting to blow out another set of candles.

At my encouragement, Dad tentatively signed up for the trial and was allocated to the group receiving combined chemotherapy and immunotherapy. Once we knew this, we rationalised that we'd adopt a 'hit it once and hit it hard' mentality, then aim for some kind of maintenance program, which—in Dad's mind—would be full of wheatgrass, meditation and the types of alternative and complementary therapies he tended to favour before he received a life-limiting diagnosis.

Treatment goals

Many of us assume that the ultimate goal of treatment is cure. While this is often the case (or perhaps the hope), in a terminal or even chronic disease setting it's worth getting clear on what the goal of treatment is up front.

Sometimes you are indeed looking to **cure or fix the issue.** In a cancer setting this is called going into remission, but to give you a less serious example, this is like being prescribed antibiotics for a bacterial infection like bronchitis. You treat the infection with the goal of curing it.

Other times you're simply looking to **improve symptoms for better quality of life.** Let's use the example of asthma. You might be prescribed an inhaler to be used in the case of an attack or to prevent one. The goal isn't to cure the asthma but to manage it and prevent it from causing harm. That isn't to say the asthma will never be cured, but that's not the *goal* of that treatment.

And then there are the times when you're looking to buy comfort or time—to **slow symptom or disease progression** or perhaps delay poor quality of life or even death. This might be the case in something like Parkinson's disease, where treatment is trying to stave off the impact of the disease and its symptoms, which—at the time of writing—can't be 'cured'.

In Dad's case I knew we were never treating to cure, although I think we were all secretly hopeful we'd be the exception to the rule. Treatment was instead aiming to slow disease progression, improve symptom control and buy time. Sometimes you're looking to achieve more than one treatment goal, and there are plenty of people who have been told the goal is management or slowing disease progression but are no doubt secretly hoping for a cure. That's more than okay. The key is to know *why* your loved one is receiving a certain treatment so you can manage both of your expectations and—as best you can—your emotional states.

Making treatment decisions

For all our medical and scientific advancement, we're still largely treating the disease rather than the person with it. One of the benefits of having Next of Kin as an advocate and carer is that they bring to the table their deep understanding of the patient, and the person they are outside of their illness or injury. Treatments need to be carefully weighed against the person's life, and Next of Kin know what's important to that person better than anyone.

If you or someone you love is faced with a treatment decision, here are some sources you'll want to tap into to make informed decisions:

- **The experts:** Specialists—like oncologists—for example—tend to deal with a particular illness or injury day in, day out. Their job is to give you your options, but they're not really meant to influence your decision—which is hard when you're feeling lost and looking for guidance from people who know what they're talking about. If they're being too neutral and won't give you their opinion so as not to influence your decision, you can ask questions like: 'If you were me, what would you do?' or 'If this was your dad, what would you be telling him to do?' That allows them to be more personal and hypothetical. If you don't like their advice, get a second opinion and a third, fourth and fifth if you need to. If patterns in the advice emerge, that's great intelligence which will help you make a more informed decision. And if you have multiple people saying the same thing, you can rest assured you're getting good advice, even if it's not what you want to hear.

- **The evidence:** To the public, it feels like science moves quickly thanks to the health headlines we see and hear in our rapid-fire, 24/7 news cycle. But evidence comes together slowly and takes a long time to trickle down from publication to practice — often many years. Without doing an academic literature review, the fastest and I think smartest way to arm yourself with the evidence is to ask your doctors if there are any good scientific papers, articles, podcast episodes or results of clinical trials they can point you towards. And (for those who don't speak fluent medicine) ask if they can summarise the headlines of what the body of evidence shows. A general practitioner (GP) or particularly health-literate friend might be better placed to do this with you than a time-poor specialist, but specialists still have to give you enough time to make you feel satisfied you've got the information you need. To get a sense of where their field of medicine has come from or might be going, you could ask questions like: 'Has the thinking around treatment of [condition] changed in the time you've been practising?' and 'Are there any new treatments on the horizon we might explore in the future or any clinical trials you're aware of?'

- **The experience:** Lived experience is invaluable. While no two healthcare journeys are the same, speaking to someone who lives with the same illness or injury, has had the same treatment or gone through the same experience will hold value in a way the experts can't deliver. It's like riding a bike: the experts have read lots of books on riding bikes and watched lots of others riding, but only people with lived experience have actually ridden one. Depending on your challenge, accessing those people may not be easy, so ask your doctors whether there are patient networks you might connect with; failing that, you can hunt online or ask friends if they know of anyone you could reach out to. This is where social media communities can be goldmines of connection and support. They can also be noisy digital caves for keyboard warriors with pent-up anger and nowhere else to direct it, so be aware of that going in.

Sometimes, making treatment decisions is easy. To use our previous example of a bacterial infection, prescribed antibiotics are likely to clear it up. But other times, making treatment decisions isn't so straightforward. It's about weighing benefit and risk, and sometimes that's clear as mud.

Here's an easy-to-use decision-making matrix to help get you started. Think of this as the baseline of information you need.

1. What treatment options are available to me?
2. For each option, what are the potential benefits and how likely are they to occur?
3. For each option, what are the potential risks and how likely are they to occur?
4. What happens if we do nothing? (We often forget that just waiting and watching is an option that's available to us.)

Once you have that information, you can look at each option and consider it in the context of the person's unique needs and objectives. Only then can you begin to make an informed decision.

Treatment tips

Before I lost Dad, I asked him what advice he'd give others navigating treatment. Here's what he said:

1. Take someone with you to appointments—don't try to handle it all alone.
2. Get help with the admin side of things. If you know you are crap at research, for example, get help early.
3. I would've valued advice from someone living with my condition early on to find out what they were doing that was working and, while I know everyone's journey is unique, to speak with someone having a similar experience. I didn't find that person, but it's possible I would have if I'd kept pushing for it.
4. Ask for what you want and need on every level. No matter how much of a people-pleaser you've been throughout your life, now is not the time for that.

Here's my advice from a Next of Kin's perspective:

1. I'd highly recommend voice recording your appointments (most smartphones can do it) so you can listen back later, just remember to ask permission up front. If they say no, tell them you'd like to be provided with detailed notes of the appointment, written in lay terms, and see how fast they change their tune. Failing that, take copious notes. AI (artificial intelligence) is starting to help bridge the gap here, often taking notes for doctors—if so, ask for a copy.
2. Doctors are not gods, even when they're world-class. I've interviewed hundreds of them and can tell you they all fail, falter and flub things sometimes. Not because they're bad, but because they're human. As such, you'll need to give them

(continued)

some grace and, occasionally, some grief. You're looking for a partner in care; make sure it's someone you think knows their stuff and that you like or, at the very least, respect.

3. When they say the system is patient-led, they are not mucking around. It's patient-led, patient-driven and patient-navigated. As such, the most important person to empower is ... you guessed it, the patient. The way to do that, as Next of Kin, is to be their co-pilot. You're not in charge; you're walking beside them and holding their hand, advocating where needed or wanted, and supporting where required. To use a *Top Gun* analogy—they're Maverick, you're Goose. And if you're too young to understand what that means ... firstly, congratulations on your high levels of natural collagen, and secondly, do yourself a favour and watch *Top Gun*. It's a classic.

All white

Dad and I are in a bright, white lounge. It's the kind of place you see in the movies where people get chemotherapy, but in real life it's ... whiter. Everything is white. White walls, floors, chairs. It feels so calm in here that it's like time has slowed down or doesn't exist. Most of the treatment chairs are empty, and if we hadn't just seen other people in the waiting room it might feel like we'd broken in after hours. I can't hear anything outside of this space; we're in a hospital, but I can't make out any alarms or call bells, or even hospital workers talking to each other nearby. The light, mainly artificial but with a touch of natural coming from a window at the end of the room, is in such high definition that I can see a piece of dust dancing from somewhere above me and I follow it with my eyes as it lands on my knee. I wish we could be as carefree as that piece of dust.

Dad is doing his best impression of a human pincushion and I feel every prick and pop. Luckily, Dad has excellent veins. 'Perfect veins for a junkie,' he'd often tell me. Dad is connected to a bag of fluid via a port in one of his perfect veins; aside from a nurse stopping by every now and again to check we're okay and to switch bags when they are empty, we're largely left to our own devices. We talk about everything and nothing, and I take a photo of Dad on my phone—he pulls a funny face to show he's tackling treatment with the same playfulness he approaches life. I don't remember it taking a long time, but I know we are there for hours. They pump the chemotherapy drugs into him first, followed by the immunotherapy drugs. A girl I went to high school with sees us and comes over to say hello—she's a nurse there and heading off for her lunch break. I get the sense Dad is annoyed that even in this most private of places it's possible to bump into people we know.

When the treatment is finished, we slowly pack up our things and make our way out of the white lounge. No one makes a fuss, walks us out or tells us what comes next. They just take out the needle, put a Band-Aid on the site like it was a quick blood test and not multiple litres of poison, and tell us we can go. It's kind of like leaving a drive-through car wash—the machines stop and you just drive away. We get as far as the lobby when Dad stops to rejig the small bag containing his belongings: a book to read, a book to write in and an annoying green water bottle that doesn't fit in the holder of his car and falls over on the wooden floorboards of his apartment dozens of times a day, scaring the bejeezus out of us. He says his arm feels wet and as I trace a line from his elbow to his fingers with my eyes I see bright red blood pouring from somewhere in the sleeve of his jacket, down his fingertips and onto the floor. It's like he has been maimed in an accident—so much red in contrast to so much white. He holds his bloodied hand in the air in front of him, I suppose in the hope that keeping the arm bent might stem the flow.

He looks around and with no one official-looking to be seen, gently makes his way past the line of people waiting to check into the white palace to alert the receptionist. She tells him to go to the back of the line. My blood boils at the same pace as the blood escaping from his arm onto the floor. I search for someone else who can help, mainly because my heart has broken a little at seeing Dad sent to the back of the queue, but also because I'm sure that whoever is in charge here would prefer he get sorted quickly rather than continue creating a small swimming pool of very red blood on their very white floor. I finally find someone who I convince to take us back through to the treatment area and clean him up so we can be on our way, take two—him in discomfort and us both in disbelief.

After just two rounds of active treatment (meaning two sessions in the white palace), Dad was so sick from side effects he was removed from the clinical trial we'd hoped would answer our prayers. Conventional treatment clearly wasn't working for Dad, even though the chemotherapy and immunotherapy *was* effective in shrinking the tumours. Did that buy us more time? Probably. But was it worth it, and if given the chance, would he choose the same again? I asked him.

'Probably not, no. I'd just party…' he tells me, both of us giggling at his half-truth.

'I felt like a little green man sitting in the corner, like I had nothing to say or contribute. It very quickly became clear it [the treatment] was highly toxic to me and not something I wanted to keep doing.'

So, after a fast and furious foray into active treatment, including some radiation to shrink tumours near his ribcage that were causing pain, Dad decided to cease treatment altogether. But the residual effects would last far beyond the final bag of cancer-fighting drugs being hung. Some would last the rest of his life—with his gut and tastebuds never the same, and neuropathy (weakness, numbness and pain from nerve damage) in his feet that went from feeling like he was walking on sponges to feeling like he was walking on broken glass.

Watching him go through treatment didn't involve the incessant throwing up we have become familiar with in Hollywood movies. Instead, I witnessed a rapid deconstruction of the very essence of his wellbeing, leaving him with a frailty I'd never seen before in my 100+ kilogram, six-foot-three dad. As his advocate, I made it my job to guide him through our fragmented healthcare system, but guiding someone to places you've never been is like finding a new location without a map, choosing directions willy-nilly based on street names and your intuition. Questions like 'What would I do?' and 'What would I want?' were on high rotation in my head, even though I knew they were near-impossible to answer on behalf of someone facing their mortality.

An imperfect system

As though it was the 1980s and not 2021, hard-copy letters confirming Dad's hospital appointments would arrive in the post sometimes (and sometimes not). I marvelled at the labour and cost required to send hard-copy appointment reminders—surely it would be easier and more cost-effective to confirm appointments via text or email, with less room for error when we would inevitably lose the letter amid the chaos of life, or change addresses. When the letters wouldn't arrive and we were unsure of next steps, there was no chance of getting through to the clinic's phone to confirm either. It was as though the clinic's reception was entirely unstaffed, even though whenever we were there the desk always seemed to have four people sitting behind the very phones I assumed we were ringing.

We'd wait for hours in the clinic, sometimes to be told the doctor had left for the day without seeing us, reasons unknown and uncommunicated. When we did see a doctor, most often it was someone new to the oncology field, with little mesothelioma experience. Or we'd get a cranky, overworked and over-it dinosaur who hadn't had the time, bandwidth or bother to get across the very fundamentals of Dad's case. There was little oversight, monitoring or observation, and almost no consistency of care. We left the clinic feeling like we were in good hands on a few rare occasions, usually after we'd seen a senior clinician (known as a consultant), but most often we left feeling like we were entirely on our own.

So, we did the best we could and muddled through. Here's how.

#1: Using the public hospital system

We used the public hospital system for diagnosis and treatment, as well as some macro-oversight of Dad's condition. Dad didn't have private health insurance so the private system wasn't available to us, but because of Western Australia's high concentration of mesothelioma, the public system was well set up to support him. The respiratory (lung) and oncology (cancer) clinics managed Dad's diagnosis and treatment, but in terms of oversight of how Dad's cancer was tracking, the departments seemingly didn't communicate well (or at all) with one another. So, we gathered the data (scans, reports, test results) from each clinic and tried to metaphorically stitch them together ourselves to understand their meaning. We took everything printed out to our appointments with a list of questions. We asked the doctors to help us make sense of Dad's disease progression by comparing previous scans and reports with the latest results to paint a picture of where we were currently. Prior to this experience, I assumed this would be done on our behalf so that all the healthcare professionals we were working with would be across Dad's case, but instead it was us who had to be across the details and often get *them* across them too.

In Chapter 1, I talked about the differences between the private and public healthcare systems. If we were in the private system, Dad would likely have had an oncologist he built a relationship with and saw consistently, and if they weren't available for any reason, his case would've been handed over to a well-trained colleague. In the public system, we saw anyone and everyone; the world-leading professor I spoke about at the top of this chapter (who told me off) once, then another consultant a few times, then maybe three or four other, far less effective colleagues at very different stages of their career. In short, there was no consistency. We had to *be* the consistency. That annoyed us, but it's a good example of learning to work within the system rather than raging against the machine. Because no one will be more driven to get good care and good results than you.

#2: Building a great relationship with a GP

We cultivated a relationship with a great GP to take on the micro or week-to-week side of things: prescribing medications and managing any simultaneous conditions or side effects, as well as being a more frequent touchpoint of care within the community (outside of our clinic visits at the hospital). When Dad was first diagnosed, he had a male GP he adored that he'd drive 30 minutes to see. Sadly, he retired early in the piece, which—while it was a shame to lose the historical rapport—gave us an opportunity to find someone closer to home with palliative care training. We met her via our aged care service provider (more on that next) when she came to Dad's apartment to do an initial 'hospice at home' intake appointment. She asked if we had a good GP and, when we said we were between GPs, said she could take on Dad's care. She made herself available even when she wasn't. She would occasionally come to Dad's home to save us coming to the clinic, and she never charged him, bulk-billing him instead. The day after Dad died, she came over to do his official cause of death certificate, and I had more than one phone conversation with her along the way where she made space for my tears and fears and buoyed me with kind words. We were so grateful for her.

#3: Choosing a service provider for supportive care

The systems supporting you will differ depending on where you live. But when you are ill or injured in Australia, you can access one of two schemes to help provide your care:

- My Aged Care (for people 65 and above, above 50 if they identify as Aboriginal or Torres Strait Islander, or if they are experiencing or at risk of homelessness). Dad was eligible for this because he was diagnosed at 66.
- NDIS (National Disability Insurance Scheme—for people under the age of 65).

The purpose of these schemes is to empower people affected by illness, injury or age to more fully participate in life and live independently in their own homes for longer. They provide funding to cover things like:

- **Personal and clinical care:** Bathing, dressing, grooming, hygiene, nursing and other therapies at home.
- **Mobility support and home maintenance:** Equipment like wheelchairs, shower rails, ramps and hospital beds, plus jobs around the home you can no longer do such as small repairs, plumbing, gardening and cleaning. A fortnightly cleaner can make the world of difference and take one thing off your plate!
- **Dietary and social support:** Nutrition, meal preparation and meal delivery services, as well as transport to appointments and help staying connected to the community.
- **Respite care:** Someone to come and be with your person for a few hours so you can go and do something for yourself. Dad hated feeling like he was being babysat by a stranger, so I'd give this person random jobs instead.

What I can tell you is this: much of our care industry isn't rewarding people sufficiently to make care their career. As a result, lots of employees at these organisations don't seem to be there for the long haul, so they have high staff turnover. I found myself frequently dealing with people who weren't wholeheartedly dedicated to delivering an exceptional customer experience. That said, I found a couple of gems along the way who were angels working within a strained system, so I think the best way forward is to know — again — you'll need to drive the ship and work *with* them to get the best support for you and your person. It won't be perfect and you might have to crack the whip (nicely) on occasion, but if you engage these services effectively they can be very, very useful. And unless you have unlimited resources, they're essential.

To get this support in place, a hospital social worker organised what's called an ACAT (Aged Care Assessment Team) assessment for us. An assessor then came to Dad's home and did an assessment of his condition and needs. They wanted to understand who lived with him (no one), who else was on hand to provide regular support (mainly me but also a small handful of others), how his apartment was set up (stairs or lift, bath or shower, any trip hazards to navigate) and what support he felt he needed. Based on your needs, you get allocated a package at a particular level, ranging from basic to high-level care. The level dictates how much funding you get.

When I say 'get', think of this more as theoretical pocket money you never actually see but do get to access indirectly. It is an annualised set of funds that gets unlocked as the months go by and becomes available not to you, but to your chosen provider—one company that delivers all the different services you require. So for argument's sake (and easy math), if you are allocated $12 000 for the year in your package, you don't receive a $12 000 bucket of money in your bank account; instead, $1000 becomes available to your service provider each month that your case worker or care coordinator can use to book in the services you require, as dictated by your package. For example, Dad's package included something like two hours of cleaning and two hours of respite care per fortnight, plus an occupational therapy assessment to inform what equipment he needed at home, and the supply of that equipment once he had accrued enough funds. For example, Dad needed a comfortable chair that was electric so it could both lay flat for him to sleep in and (eventually) to help him stand up. Purchasing the chair would have exceeded the funds available, so our care coordinator helped us hire one instead—at a significantly lower cost than purchasing one. You're trying to match need with timing and budget, and it's a bit of a dance.

Once you have your assessment and your package, you then engage a service provider (I share a link to a tool in the Resources section at the back of this book that is designed to help you choose one). I found the tool—while useful—quite overwhelming. It breaks down who all the registered providers are, and what they charge and offer, but if you don't have any contextual experience with which to evaluate this information then the detail may not mean much to you, making it hard to choose. Any provider you're interested in will likely send someone to meet with you who is well versed in their packages (and usually has some sales skills; it's a crowded market, so their job is to sign you as a client). They all have different fee structures, so it's worth doing your homework and asking other carers who they use. This is a big task, but one worth investing some time in. Remember that while some are not-for-profit organisations, many are still big businesses and some charge big fees, meaning much less of your funding ends up being available for your person.

Dad was already under something called 'hospice at home' through one of the big providers, and we were encouraged to stick with them so everything was under one umbrella and we weren't dealing with multiple providers. We were told this provider was the best in the business, and I don't have anything to compare it to, but admittedly the experience left a fair bit to be desired. The trouble, I suppose, is that you don't know what you don't know, but if I had my time again I'd probably pick 3–5 providers I liked the look of and then invest some time in meeting with each of them to compare their offerings. I am reluctant to paint all care providers with our experience. It's possible that others may not face the same staffing challenges that were evident to me with ours. And this is why you need to do your homework.

#4: Engaging a doula

We engaged a death doula to walk beside us through Dad's death and deliver spiritual and administrative guidance. She also happened to be a nurse with 25 years' palliative care experience, which thrilled the science-loving, anti-woo-ist in me, giving us someone to call to thrash out anything that came our way. While Dad wasn't overly receptive to the spiritual guidance side of things, especially in the beginning (preparing for death, envisioning a 'good' death, talking about what he wanted after his death), the support our doula offered me, both spiritually and administratively, was invaluable. (I talk more about her in Part 4.)

#5: Connecting with a support group

We connected with a local support group for guidance informed by lived experience. Again, Dad didn't really want to dip into this support and kept his distance (even though you might recall he said he would've found value in speaking to someone with his condition). I suspect he resisted out of fear of it illuminating what his future might look (or feel) like. But the support this group gave me, especially via one of their staff (who had lost her husband to the same disease and cared for many others as a nurse), was vital to my survival. I am so grateful for them, and particularly for her. Being able to lean on someone who has 'been there' is the closest thing you'll find to a compass in the wilderness.

Hindsight is a valuable thing. What would we have done differently if we had our time again? I'd have pushed for immunotherapy only, which is kind of like training your own immune system to be an attack dog for cancer cells. Chemotherapy is still a vital tool in the cancer toolkit, especially given immunotherapy doesn't work in all cancers (yet), but it's the medical equivalent of weedkiller—it kills everything in its path, whether good (healthy cells) or bad (cancer cells). After seeing what it did to Dad, encouraging chemotherapy is one of my biggest regrets.

As for Dad, when I asked what he would do if he had his time again, he said he didn't know what he'd do differently. What I saw him do—things that, if I had to guess, he'd stand by and possibly dial up—was make changes to what he ate (less sugar and junk) and drank (no coffee and less booze). And as he slowly recovered from the treatment he did have, we were gifted two precious years where Dad was happy(ish), healthy(ish) and here—time we'll be forever grateful for. Until eventually, the disease caught up, spreading faster than we could contain it.

CHAPTER 4

In the pocket

In his youth, and I suppose to a lesser extent for much of his life, my dad was an addict. In his twenties speed was his drug of choice until he met smoother, sexier heroin. Dad always said he was grateful to heroin; without it, he didn't think he'd have been able to overcome his addiction to speed, which in his opinion and experience was a far more dangerous drug. Bear in mind it was the 1970s and 1980s, when—from what I understand—the drugs were a different beast to what they are today. Purer, cleaner, but still capable of wreaking havoc on someone's life.

While Dad would spend a lifetime leaning heavily on his favourite crutches—the attention of women, red wine, nicotine and the occasional dabble in something more exciting—me coming along was for the most part a wake-up call to clean up his act. He was moderately successful at getting clean, I think, outside of the time he got high while looking after me, forgot I was there and took himself to the local public pool for a dip. Mum got home from work to find an unsupervised baby, and Dad got home after his swim to find his belongings on the lawn. Even so, while he'd be the first to admit he still had some substance-reliance issues and less-than-ideal behaviours, his addictions had—by and large—been put to bed in his latter decades. Which is why it was heartbreaking to see them return in his final months of life.

I can't remember who suggested fentanyl as a potential opiate for Dad. It's very possible it was me. The morphine-based drugs he'd been prescribed to manage his pain and breathlessness made him feel 'smacky, like a junkie nodding off on a train', he said, so at some point someone suggested we try fentanyl. I'd read about the fentanyl crisis overseas, particularly in the US, where folded-over 'zombies' roamed the streets and occasionally ate people's faces off (I might've conflated that last bit, but it might also be true). But—I reasoned to myself—this was clean fentanyl. Medical-grade. Doctor-approved. Surely the chances of addiction were lower—and besides, if he *did* become an addict again for the limited time he had left, was that the worst thing in the world? He was dying. There wasn't time for him to throw in the towel on his life and take up with the actual junkies camped at the end of his urban street.

Fentanyl is a rapid-acting synthetic opiate with pain-relieving properties considered 100 times more potent than morphine and 50 times more potent than heroin, which is why it is given to people with terminal cancer diagnoses. I suppose, like many addictions, this one of Dad's was good until it wasn't. In the beginning, it *was* kind of a miracle drug, putting wind in his sails where there was none. I could see the lift in him when he was 'on'; it was obvious fentanyl made him feel like he could get out and about, have conversations with people and live his life a little bit—and no one would deny him that, even if it was artificial. If you didn't know he was dying, you'd just assume he was a slightly dishevelled, slow-walking man in too-big pants.

Over a short period of time, Dad had doubled, then tripled, his fentanyl use. It was always with his doctor's approval, but likely off-label (the term doctors use to describe prescribing a drug or treatment that's approved but then applied outside of its typical, recommended way). As per the law of gravity, what goes up must come down, and as Dad's use increased, the high of the drug was followed by a fairly nasty downside of anxiety and panic. When he used it sporadically or lightly, this downside was minimal. But when his use increased, so did his anxiety. Before we knew it, the window of time he spent feeling good in 'the pocket' was outweighed by the time he spent coming down. If we were driving, I'd have to pull over so he could get out of the car and put his bare feet on the earth to ground himself. If children were around, I could see his anxiety levels rising in line with the amount of noise they were making. And the rest of the time, I'd see him doing almost constant mental arithmetic as to how he could lift himself up—to see if he could pharmacologically fashion the feeling of being someone who wasn't dying.

For a while we were a well-oiled, albeit broken, machine. Overnight, as a result of lying down for so long, fluid would build up in Dad's lungs. So, every morning he'd wake to severe breathlessness and panic, which he'd use over-the-counter cough medication, oxygen and a nebuliser to bring under control. Then, his stomach would evacuate the fluid that had accumulated overnight, causing a 20–30-minute period of retching uncontrollably into a red bucket we kept perpetually beside his bed (kind of like when you've had a big night but have nothing other than bile and a few mouthfuls of too-late water in your stomach to bring up). By the time this hour-long process had finished, Dad was ready to have his breakfast and medications to mark the official start of the day and his relentless pursuit of the pocket. And I would commence my role as both witness and beneficiary of the rollercoaster that comes with chasing a high.

Good cop, bad cop

One of the myriad challenges of being a carer is that there are times you get to be good cop and times you have to be bad cop, sometimes both at once to different people. Your job as the patient advocate is to help them communicate their wants, but when their wants go against their clinical need (for example), you're put in a difficult situation and—as the closest person to them—can find yourself in the firing line.

Dad had always said that when I couldn't manage his care at home anymore, he'd go into hospice. I initially felt honoured he trusted me to make that call on his behalf, but eventually the decision weighed on me—I was charged with having to make him do something he didn't want to do (go into hospice) because it's what *I* needed. Cue guilt on steroids and me holding on for dear life to keep him at home for as long as possible until I was so worried about his safety—and so depleted in terms of my own self-care—that I felt we had no choice but for Dad to go into hospice.

Caring for Dad had been a crash course in just how sick people can get. With every month that passed for probably the final year, I couldn't believe he was still with us. *How much sicker can he get?!* I asked myself frequently in my head (and sometimes even aloud when Dad was out of earshot). To which the answer from the universe was always: *Much, much sicker than this.* Dad was fearful that going into hospice meant he was dying imminently. It's what we think we know: palliative care is for people who are dying, and hospice is where people go to die. But palliative care has had a rebrand. It's now called supportive care, and the evidence is clear that engaging supportive care earlier can lead to more time and better quality of life, whether someone is dying or not. Our amazing doula taught me that hospice isn't a one-way street (as in, you can go in and come out again) and that the aim with end-of-life care is to ensure symptoms (such as pain and breathlessness) are well controlled. Hospice, she said, would help us achieve that.

A call bell, 24/7 nursing staff plus daily doctor oversight, as well as what I thought would be some respite for me, were the leverage we needed to get Dad to agree to enter hospice. When a bed became available, we packed Dad's things as though he was heading away for a weekender. Some clothes, his slippers, a book, his toothbrush and his laptop so he could distract himself with a series or two. Seeing him get ready felt like I was watching a reality show of our lives. My brain kept thinking things like: *There's my dad getting ready to go to hospice. Weird.* In the short lift ride from his first-floor apartment to the ground-floor car park, he leaned forward to put his head on my chest and I could feel, as if through osmosis, that he was scared he wouldn't be coming back. I blinked back tears and said a silent prayer to the lift lights above that he was wrong before the doors opened to the next scene in our episode. The same car park we'd entered a hundred times before felt different that day, as if someone had staged it and we were simply there to act out the roles of dying father and grieving daughter.

After a short, quiet drive, I parked his truck in the car park and we walked into the hospice, holding hands as we often did. I don't know how many people walk into hospice; in the two weeks we were there, I don't think I saw anyone not wheeled inside in a hospital bed or wheelchair. It felt like we could be in the wrong place. The hospice was startlingly clean, light and bright, like the interior designer had been given the brief of 'hospital, but make it upbeat'. The staff were smiley, the rooms opened onto gardens with tranquil water fountains, and on Friday afternoons there was a happy hour and musicians that would play piano or harp. Dad wasted no time jumping onto the harp for a photo, suggesting in his trademark dark humour we send it to his friends to suggest he'd been let into heaven after all.

In my head, Dad going into hospice would allow me to gather myself, get some sorely needed sleep and reset for what I knew was going to be the hardest leg of the journey so far. While it gave me comfort knowing he was one press of a button away from help if needed, I still didn't feel like I could leave him there alone for more than a few hours, and I made sure I or someone was there with him pretty much every minute of the day and night. He felt better when his people were around, and with time feeling increasingly limited, there was a fairly constant supply of visitors to plug any gaps. This allowed me more flexibility to get my kids to school—or I'd bring them into the hospice for the day, where they'd eat Dad's snacks and watch cartoons on my laptop, beautifully oblivious to what was going on around them.

When he entered the hospice, Dad was taking fentanyl multiple times each day. He captured every dose and time in what we called The Blue Book—a small, lined notebook I picked up from the local dollar store that he carried everywhere he went. The Blue Book allowed him to make sense of symptoms that felt out of his control. It was the master logbook to his life, his only compass in a rugged and unforgiving landscape of deteriorating health, poorly managed symptoms and a deep fear of the death that was clearly and inevitably coming. The drugs hospice doctors used to get Dad's symptoms under control made him sleepy, which felt to Dad like the beginning of the end and made him fight sleep like it was the enemy. I could smell the fear on Dad, with strong notes of distrust in his doctors and even in me whenever I tried to gently get him on board with something they were suggesting because I thought it might help him.

After an impassioned plea to the doctors that the new drugs were making him too 'out of it', we reverted to the fentanyl for additional symptom control. Before I knew it he was taking it on the hour, every hour during the day: the Trojan horse in an armoury of drugs to get Dad up, down and everything in between. There were long-acting medications to take at the same time of the day or night, which could be tweaked with some consultation to achieve their desired effect, usually lessening symptoms or helping him get to sleep. But it was the as-needed or 'breakthrough' medications that got us into trouble. Like a nutty professor, Dad obsessed over getting the delicate mix and timing of these medications just right, favouring the fentanyl above all else and making no attempt to hide his disdain for anyone — personal or professional — who suggested anything other than more and more fentanyl being the answer to whatever symptom we were trying to manage. Pain? Fentanyl. Breathlessness? More fentanyl. Headache? Perhaps more fentanyl. Anxiety? Surely more fentanyl would help. It felt kind of like using water to quench your thirst, fuel your car, feed your cat and pay your phone bill. Effective, just not for all.

Fentanyl and other drugs with high potential for abuse and addiction are tightly regulated and controlled in care settings. In order for Dad to get his dose he had to press the call bell, wait for a nurse to come and take the request, then wait while the nurse went to find another nurse to complete the process. The two nurses would have to unlock the cupboard protecting the fentanyl, get it out, do the paperwork and bring it to Dad. This process could take between 15 and 45 minutes depending on what else was happening on the ward, which made it very difficult for Dad to stay in 'the pocket' given he was taking it hourly. If they took too long, I'd watch him get more and more agitated, silently cursing the nurses, their children and their children's children. And god help any poor soul who dared imply it could be the enough-to-lift-a-small-cow-off-the-ground levels of fentanyl that were making him feel anxious, speedy and panicked. Suggesting any other tactic (say, occasionally interspersing the fentanyl with an anxiety-quelling medication) was social suicide, with Dad's mood becoming progressively harder to manage.

And the most frequent bad cop? Me. All of a sudden, Dad started having moments of feeling like I wasn't on his side because I was gently encouraging him to lessen his use — I was the one metaphorically standing between him and his precious drug. Every day felt like a dozen tiny heartbreaks as I watched him realise the once-miracle drug was no longer effective against the silent assassin that was his disease, and it was time to change tack.

What it means to be an advocate

Advocacy is defined as the act or process of supporting a cause or proposal. It could be silent advocacy, like voting or signing a petition. Or it could be more active or verbal, speaking up on behalf of someone or something's needs when you feel passionate about it or when they are unable or less able to do it for themselves. You might advocate for a cause like LGBTQIA+ rights in your community, or for your neurodiverse child to get the support they need from the education and healthcare systems. Advocacy is essentially going in to bat for a team — your team — whether you choose it or it chooses you. In a medical setting, advocacy can feel like you're performing a carefully balanced tightrope walk, holding the fingertips of the person you're caring or advocating for on one hand, and a plethora of fingertips from many, many hands in the other.

In my experience, there are two key parts to advocacy:

1. Being clear on exactly what you're advocating for (the goal)
2. Having the knowledge and literacy, as well as the communication and negotiation skills, to achieve that goal (the outcome).

These are high-level, executive functions in any setting. They don't come naturally to all of us, or even to most of us. But they're worth investing some time in, as you'll use the skill again and again both personally and professionally—whether you're advocating for a cause, a person or yourself.

Getting clear on what you're advocating for

Imagine going to a football match. The players enter the field, the crowd goes wild. The siren sounds and the ball starts flying around, players passing it deftly back and forth as they shift it from one end of the field towards the other. When they get there, you see them looking around, confused. You realise it's because there are no goalposts, so they don't know what they're aiming for or what constitutes a goal, much less a win. Not being clear on what you're advocating for is the equivalent but—depending on the situation—may have much higher stakes.

Being clear on the goal is vital, and the hardest part is that the person we're advocating for:

- May not know what they want
- May not be able to communicate what they want (physically or emotionally)
- May change what they want over time
- May know what they want in theory and then find out it's not actually what they want when faced with the reality.

Communication here is critical. It's often not a one-and-done conversation, but rather a series of discussions that evolve our understanding of what someone wants or needs and, as such, what we are advocating for. You know your person best; if they've never been good at talking about hard things, it's unlikely they're going to start now. Facing illness is like putting ourselves under a magnifying glass—we usually become more of whatever we already were. If we're grumpy, we get grumpier. If we're introverted, we get more introverted. And if we're fiercely independent, we try to stay fiercely independent.

Knowing how to advocate for someone you love is a combination of understanding them and how they operate, and communicating with them about their wants and needs so you don't have to operate on guesswork.

How this works in reality will vary wildly depending on your situation. Here are some questions you might consider asking your person before you go into an important appointment with them.

- **'Hey, how are you feeling going into this?'** Are they nervous? Agitated? Overwhelmed? Hopeful? This will help you manage their emotional state, or at the very least manage your own in the face of it.

- **'What are you wanting to get out of this appointment?'** This is the most powerful question of all, because it allows you to set a clear intention for what you're hoping to achieve, and then to feel a sense of success or at least know when you have achieved that. For example, they might want to achieve a greater understanding of their treatment options, find out the answer to a very specific question, get a particular symptom under control or request a referral to someone. Knowing the answer to this question before you go in, and remaining flexible if what you/they want is not achievable in that appointment for whatever reason, will help you know if the appointment has been valuable and effective.

- **'Do you feel up to chatting to the doctors? Do you want me to contribute, or do you just want me to be there in support and let you run the show?'** This is about understanding their expectations of how you'll behave. They may not know the answer, but if they do, that's a valuable guide as to how you should act. Do they need you to ask the hard questions? Act as their memory? Just be moral support? For some, being spoken for feels diminishing. But others might be grateful to not have to come up with the words.

Getting the balance of adding value but not overstepping is a dance; they're leading, you're following, unless you're in a legal or literal position where they're unable to advocate for themselves and need you to do so for them. The person the healthcare professionals most need to hear from is the patient, but you also hold valuable clues to their experience because you've been watching on, as if through a window. You're also likely to be the one remembering details of appointments and implementing any suggestions, which is why you need to understand (and be able to recall or capture) the details.

Sometimes advocacy is out loud, and sometimes it's knowing when to be quiet. But you are always, always in pursuit of the goal. This means knowing clearly what the goal is at any given moment, and knowing that as you progress through the journey, it's highly likely to change.

Having the skills to achieve that goal

There are a few core skills that are essential to being an advocate. The first is having some knowledge and literacy around what you're advocating for. You're probably full bottle on your person, but you also need to know about their illness or injury. Knowledge is power here. While you'll never know as much as the experts, having a sense of what they're talking about can help you find efficiency (so they have to explain less and you can get through more in limited appointment time) and shows you're a capable partner in care. It'll also make appointments less overwhelming and easier to understand. Think about it this way: if you were starting a new job in a new industry, you'd do some research. This is no different, so get at least a baseline of knowledge so you can speak the language. The internet is the best place for that these days, so if you aren't tech-savvy, ask for help from someone who is.

Next, let's talk communication skills. I've alluded to this a lot so far, but communication skills are critical to advocating for ourselves or anyone else. We all like to be liked, and this is one of those situations where you get more flies with honey than you do with vinegar. Here's what I know about most healthcare professionals:

- They usually went into health because they like people and want to help them. This is especially true of nurses but broadly applicable to most.

- The systems they work within are strained, which can make their jobs difficult.
- Depending on the setting, they are often dealing with people experiencing high levels of stress. This is the reason you might see signs in clinic waiting rooms or hospitals saying 'abuse towards our staff will not be tolerated' or something similar — which are there for a reason.

If we hold these realities in mind, what can help you get a better result is:

- **If they like you.** Remember their name, look them in the eye and smile when you see them. Ask how they are, how their family is, holiday was or even weekend was. They're human, just like you. Connect with them on a human level.
- **If they respect you.** Show them you've done the work. If you've done some reading or research, tell them. If you've been doing the exercises they recommended, let them know. Again, show them you're an active and willing participant in care.
- **If you help make their job easier.** If I was to ask you how much water you drank or how many times you went to the toilet yesterday, would you know the answer? Capturing some data can be incredibly helpful for doctors and give them a clearer picture of what's going on that doesn't rely on flawed memory. You don't have to journal every cough, sneeze and fart, but taking some notes each day can be valuable for tracking symptoms or evaluating how a medication is working, for example. Apps can help (I use the Notes app in my smartphone, broken down by date so I can orient myself), but a pen-and-paper notebook (if you can make sense of it easily) or calendar is just as good. If you're advocating for someone else, tell them you're taking notes along the way to help in appointments. Don't spring it on them in front of the doctor, as they'll feel like you've been secretly keeping tabs on them.
- **If you give them some grace.** Doctors often run late. Their rooms are filled with unknowns and as such their days can

be filled with delays. They may be seeing patients while simultaneously managing oversight of other patients at another clinic or hospital, checking results or having their own life issues. Maybe their child is sick, they are caring for an ageing parent or they are struggling with their mental health. They don't run late for fun, so go prepared to wait and then give them some grace when you have to. They'll appreciate it and you'll get a better result if you don't go in pissed off.

- **If you are clear, direct and honest.** If you have a goal, tell them what it is up front. You can say something like: 'What we'd love to achieve in this appointment is X, do you think that's possible?' Then they can manage your expectations accordingly. When they ask you questions, answer clearly and succinctly. They'll ask for more information if they want it. Be honest; don't make anything seem better or worse than it is. Doctors are often trying to juggle any test results you've got, how you're presenting to them (as in, how you or the patient looks and seems), what you're telling them and what they know about your condition, plus keeping in mind your unique situation. It's a lot to filter into a 15- or even 30-minute appointment. You get very little time with them, so use it wisely.

- **If you thank them for their care.** At the end of every appointment, thank them sincerely for their care and time. The goal is for them to walk away genuinely liking you. If they do, they may be more likely to go above and beyond for you if and when you need them to.

The aim here is building strong relationships, and that requires some effort.

Not all healthcare professionals are created equal

All the above being said, I need to acknowledge a universal truth here, which is that—like any other industry—there are amazing practitioners, mediocre practitioners and bloody awful practitioners. They get into medical school based on their good grades, not their exceptional personalities, and while some people are happy to forgo communication skills for smarts, I'd rather work with healthcare professionals who have both. These unicorns exist, and while finding the right ones can take some time, here are some easy red flags to avoid:

- **If you don't feel seen or heard.** You've done the work to get clear on your goal, conveyed it clearly and don't feel like they're listening. Feel free to say it again—slower, clearer and more direct. If you still aren't getting what you need, ask them to be clearer with you. It's okay to say something like: 'I feel like I'm not being heard here. Can we start again?'

- **If they don't respect your time.** I stand by what I said earlier in terms of giving them some grace. But if you feel like they always run late, never apologise for keeping you waiting and then make you feel rushed while you're there—like you're taking up too much of their precious time—you're in the wrong place. However, remember that you have more latitude with who you see in the private system than the public system, so you may need to be realistic about your strategy if you're in the public system or come up with some ways to work better with who is available to you (such as the strategies we're discussing in this chapter).

- **If they doctor-speak you.** This is getting rarer now, but sometimes doctors will use big, fancy medical words because it makes them feel clever. Wrapping your head around some of the terminology is a smart move, but if you don't understand them, tell them so. Say something like, 'I don't understand, can you please explain it to me again in simple terms?' Your doctors have a responsibility and duty of care to take you through your options or results to whatever level of detail you need, which is the reason you don't usually get sent results directly—they need to give them some context in terms of your unique situation. General practitioners (GPs) are great decoders and may be able to dedicate more time to going through details with you than a specialist may have available. And, know that your results belong to you. Always ask for a copy, printed or emailed, to take home with you. If you have opted in to an online record system like

My Health Record (which we have in Australia), your results should go there directly — but check to make sure that's the case and ensure you know how to access them.

A note on specialists: Doctors study hard to get into medicine, then they study hard to become doctors. Specialists then study even harder for even longer to become specialists, meaning that by the time they complete a training program and reach the highest level of consultant — essentially, the boss — they can feel pretty important. I say that with love and respect, as some of my dearest friends and colleagues are specialists. But it's worth acknowledging that getting to the top of any field (especially a competitive field like medicine) usually requires some level of ego. Couple that with our fairly chronic shortage of specialists and some can let that importance go to their big-brained heads. It's worth being aware of so you can kindly and carefully factor that into your strategy and get the best results for the person you're caring for.

- **If they belittle or bully you.** No one has the right to make you feel small, stupid or silly — not even doctors. If they do, you need to call it out, report it and find someone else right away.

- **If they don't want you to get a second opinion.** Good doctors welcome a second opinion — they're happy for someone to sense-check their thinking. Great doctors may even recommend someone to get one from and share their details with you. They're not cagey or protective of their contacts, but secure enough in their work and also in knowing they're not for everyone — you might work better with a younger doctor, a female doctor or someone with a similar cultural background to you. They just want you to get the best care.

- **If you can't get in to see them within a reasonable timeframe.** If you need primary care (so you need to see your GP quickly, for example), you need to be able to get in to see them or someone within their practice within a reasonable timeframe (usually a few days but, depending on where you live, this can be much longer — especially for those who live regionally, rurally or remotely). Specialists are harder to get appointments with and you need to use your common sense here depending on what the issue is, but if your specialist is booking nine months in advance and you need to see them sooner, it may be time to find someone else or to bust out your negotiation skills.

I am by no means a master negotiator, but here are a few things that may help you get the results you need from your healthcare professionals.

Know who the decision-maker is

Often, doctors will have a medical receptionist who holds the keys to the kingdom. If it's them you need to get on side, do so. Use your exceptional communication skills: repeat back their name, ask how they are—a little charm goes a long way. Once you have some rapport, ask for what you want. Be direct and clear. You can say things like: 'I really need to see the doctor sooner than that, can I take the appointment you're suggesting but also be put on a cancellation list in case something comes up sooner?' Then, call them every week (every day if you're desperate) to remind them you're still waiting. You can say something like: 'Just checking in to see if you've had any cancellations pop up, thanks so much for keeping me in mind Shirley, I really appreciate it.' Calling first thing in the morning is best, as they may have received a cancellation overnight (plus they hopefully haven't had their day sabotaged by unexpected events yet)—and this way, you'll be top of mind if they get a cancellation during the day. If there are any parameters here (such as days or times you know you can't do), tell them in advance. But if you can be flexible (or have the luxury of living close by so can get there quickly), then say so. The more options they have, the better. If you're lucky enough to get a cancellation, I'd move heaven and earth to take it. If they find you a cancellation and you turn it down, they may not be quick to offer you another.

If the decision-maker is the doctor and you aren't able to speak to them, ask if you're able to send an email that could be passed on. Keep it short, kind and direct—clearly lay out what you're asking for and see if you get a different result. If you're still not having any luck, it may be time to consider trying someone else. Keep your appointment for 2038 or whenever they can get you in, but actively try for others in the background. If you get in with someone else sooner, you can always cancel the other appointment. And, ask your specialist if there's anyone they'd recommend who may not have as long a wait time. Newer specialists to the game tend to have more open books. They may not have as much experience, but they have trained more recently and if you can get in to see them sooner, that's a win.

Be clear about your position, then ask for their help

Let's say you're trying to get someone you love in to see a specialist. I'd say things like: 'I'm really concerned about X [this should be an honest concern, don't hoodwink anyone], what's the best thing to do here? Is there anything you'd recommend to help us be seen sooner? I'd be grateful for your advice.' Make it personal: to them, you are one in hundreds, maybe thousands of patients. Again, try asking what they'd do if it was their parent/sibling/child/friend.

Stay calm

Very few people enjoy arguing with anyone, let alone a stranger. One of my superpowers is that when I get mad I get blisteringly calm. Ask my husband; it drives him nuts. If you're frustrated you can tell them that, but if it's not a frustration they've contributed to or caused, say that as well. For example: 'Stacey, I know this has nothing to do with you, but I feel really frustrated I was told X and now you're saying it's actually Y. I know you didn't create the problem, but I would be so appreciative if you could help me solve it…what's possible here in terms of a solution?' If they help, thank them profusely. Remember their name, and if you see them when you next go in for an appointment, thank them again in person. Now, you have an ally.

Keep your data and know your stuff

If you've made multiple calls to the same place, note down the days, times and names of who you spoke to. Being able to say, 'I spoke to

Thomas on Monday and he told me XYZ ...' is way more powerful than, 'I spoke to someone the other day ...' This helps hold them accountable when there are multiple staff, which is often the case. Again, stay calm. Be kind. Ask for their help. And if they won't give it to you, ask if there's anyone else you can talk to. We're all about solutions.

• • •

Hopefully, now you're feeling more empowered to advocate for your person, yourself or even a chosen cause. The headline, I suppose, is that you'll always get more people on side with kindness than you will by being a pain-in-the-ass. No one likes a pain-in-the-ass, and at a time when you may already be under pressure or feeling distressed, you're better off moving through the world with allies rather than enemies. This will make for a less stressful experience for both you and the person you're caring for. And care can be incredibly stressful, as I was about to learn.

PART II

Physical Care

Caring for your person and yourself (whether it's a marathon or a sprint), working with your care team, finding coping strategies and life on the frontline.

CHAPTER 5

Go team

It's been 48 hours since I've seen Dad, one of the longer stints apart we'll do in my two-and-a-half-year care tenure. I've been hosting a two-day conference, and with little downtime and much prep to do between days, I've made the difficult decision not to see him on the evening between—as well as needing to familiarise myself with the next day's notes, I really need to see my children. On the evening in question, he assures me over text he is fine, just getting lots of rest.

As soon as the conference has finished and I'm waiting for my taxi, I call him. He sounds terrible, so I tell him I'll drop my things off at home, pack a bag and come straight over. I arrive in the early evening to the last rays of sunset trickling through the windows. It's too early in the day for the house to be so quiet, and too late for no lights to be on. The apartment smells stuffy, like that smell when someone has been sleeping in a small room with not enough air. I quietly shut and lock the front door behind me, put my overnight bag down in the middle of the living room and tiptoe towards Dad's room. Having a key gives me easy access to the apartment when Dad is in bed, as he often is, but also puts me in the precarious position of scaring him when he has forgotten I am coming. If I call out from the door I risk waking him, but if I get to his bed unannounced, I risk scaring him. Sometimes I err on the side of caution and call out from the door, but he doesn't hear me so I give him a fright anyway, which gets me in trouble. It's a choose-my-own-adventure game that is pretty much lose-lose.

I walk tentatively into his room, gently say hello and find him in his bed, on his side, covered in blankets. I think it is entirely possible he hasn't left his bed in 48 hours, and he is glad I am there. He says that if I hadn't come, he feels like he would've died. I get a nurse to the house through our hospice at home service who suggests we go to the emergency department, where they will probably suggest he be admitted to hospital. Dad is desperate to avoid that and we have a pre-scheduled appointment at the hospital respiratory clinic the following day, so I convince her we can manage until then.

Dad is up retching all night. I try to get snippets of sleep but am on high alert, listening out for the next round. I sit beside him helplessly, rubbing his back occasionally and emptying the bucket when necessary. By morning, we feel like we are on our knees, praying at the altars of disease (him) and silent distress (me). If we didn't already have an appointment at the respiratory clinic, we'd have no choice but to present to the emergency department. There's only so much we can do from home and, put simply, Dad is deteriorating more quickly than my skills or spirit can keep up with.

I park the car at the hospital and we begin the short walk to the clinic, but after just a few steps Dad doubles over onto a parked car and says he can't walk any further. I run the short distance to the clinic holding our bags and ask the receptionist for a wheelchair. I must seem flustered, as a nurse asks me to point her in Dad's direction so she can retrieve him and wheel him over. I want to go and get him myself, and immediately feel guilty I don't push harder to do so. Poor Dad is going to be picked up by a stranger — a nurse half his size — and wheeled back to me, like a valet bringing my car around.

When we check in with the receptionist, she asks us to head into the main hospital building and get some images taken of Dad's chest and lungs while we wait for the respiratory doctor. It's just 'through those doors and around to the right', she says. Eventually, after a right, left, left again, down a long hallway, then left followed by a quick right, we find the reception area for the rabbit warren/imaging department. On the way we pass men shuffling with walkers, and I make up stories about them in my head—who they are, where they live, how they got here. I park Dad in the middle of the waiting room, alongside some chairs so he and his wheelchair feel like they blend in. I take the opportunity to run to the bathroom for a nervous wee and come back to see Dad slumped in the wheelchair, a husk of himself. It is the first time I remember feeling like his disease had beaten him.

At the imaging technician's request, I wheel Dad into the imaging room and into position for the machine. I stand back, beside an imaging bed that is unmade with bloodied sheets. I wonder if the imaging technician is embarrassed, like when someone comes to your house unannounced and it's messy. I wonder whether she figures that as we aren't using the bed, why would we care? I wonder if she is struggling within a system that is under pressure, even though she seems to be in a good mood and we've been brought straight through after very little wait time. She asks Dad to stand so she can take his images, and as I watch him struggle to get out of the wheelchair, I instinctively run in to help him—the way a mother would run onto a sports field to help a small child who had fallen to the ground. I hook my arms underneath his armpits from behind and gently lift him up, checking to see if he feels he can hold his position for a few seconds. He says he can so I dart out of the way, and he stands shakily while she snaps her pictures from behind the screen that protects her from absorbing non-stop radiation all day.

When she is done, he collapses into his chair and I walk over to him, carefully coming around to face him and pulling him into me as he falls apart. His head on my chest, he sobs audibly with recognition of where we are at. Where he is at. And where he won't be for much longer. 'I don't want to die,' he says. And because I know he is in fact dying and I don't know what to say, I say silly things, like, 'It's okay' (it isn't), 'I'm sorry' (I am) and 'I love you' (I do).

We gather ourselves and start the return route back to the respiratory clinic. We are asked to wait in the waiting room, but with

Dad struggling to sit up in a wheelchair that clearly wasn't made for tall people, I ask if there is a spare consulting room he might be able to lie down in. There is, so we make our way around to it and Dad lies on the bed. I read, giving him some time to rest or decompress. Before long, a young doctor comes and joins us, asks Dad a bunch of questions and — perhaps being unsure what else to do — tells Dad he'll need to be admitted to the hospital to get him more stable. I see the disappointment register on Dad's face — he hates being in hospital. Moments later the big boss comes in; Dad has seen him before and likes him, so I exhale a little. The doctor pulls up a chair, sits down so he is at Dad's eye level and leans forward, elbows on his knees and hands gently clasped together. I am watching the scene unfold as if we're at the theatre, equal parts terrified of what is about to be said and mesmerised by the bedside stagecraft playing out in front of me. The doctor is soft but firm, kind without mincing words.

'The end of this disease has a sharp decline; it's like standing on the edge of a cliff,' he tells us. 'Some people stand there for ages, and it takes a big gust of wind to knock them off. For others, it's a light breeze.'

We don't know which weather he is forecasting for us, so for the first time I can remember, Dad asks how long he has.

'Days or weeks, not months. Go home and spend time with your family, and when you can't manage at home anymore, come to the hospice.'

We leave in silence, driving past the beach on the way home because why not. I am hyper-vigilant, watching him for clues as to how the very worst news is landing. As we wind the streets on the short drive, we switch conversational gears like Formula One drivers — from death and estate planning to local architecture and the coastline. It feels, to me at least, strangely performative. My mouth is conversing, but my mind is latched onto the thought that this might be my last Monday with Dad, ever.

We decide to get my younger siblings over for dinner that night to get them up to speed. You might recall me saying in the Introduction that my family tree isn't exactly straightforward. On Dad's side, there are five of us to four different women, and let's just say none of us were planned.

To orient you, here's the lay of the land.

My older sister lives in Chicago—has done since she was three. Dad was 19 when he had her and not really ready to be a parent, so her mother re-partnered with an American and moved to Chicago, daughter in tow. While Dad would try to stay connected, it would be many years before his letters would find their way to her and many more before they'd connect in a meaningful way.

Then, there's me. Almost 10 years younger than my older sister and the daughter of two of the most physically blessed people Western Australia has birthed. No pressure.

Fifteen years later came the middle child. His mother is a glamorous import from the UK who at the time drove a white Mazda convertible and kind of looks like Minnie Driver. While her relationship with Dad didn't last, they gave it a good crack before she eventually re-partnered and moved, with my younger brother, to Broome, a town around 1700 kilometres north of Perth, again putting geographical distance between Dad and one of his children. I know this pained him but—from what I understand—he worked hard to close the gap, even moving up there for a period of time.

Four years after that came another girl, my little sister. Her mother was good to me (most of Dad's partners were) and great for Dad. He had a tendency to use the Moon for contraception, so they fell pregnant again quickly. My littlest brother arrived not much more than a year later; they battled on but, after a few years and the pressure of two children in quick succession, that relationship crumbled too.

So, at this stage, Dad has five children aged 48 to 17. He sits down with the Australian contingent to deliver bad news, again. I watch Dad carefully and bravely choose his words, and I see my siblings carefully and bravely choose their responses. No one lets the tears flow; they just nod and blink them away in an attempt to hold it together for their dad. *This is it,* I think to myself. *This is the hardest stuff life has to throw at us.* I am both grateful for my years of life experience and devastated I can't put each of my young siblings on fast-forward mode to get them to the same place.

I intrinsically know I am lucky. Dad has seen me find a career I love, walked me down the aisle into the arms of the world's kindest man and watched me become a mother, making him the proudest grandfather. There is no age that is 'good' to lose a parent, but at almost 40 it's not lost on me how fortunate I am to have had him for as long as I have. I am already grieving for all the things my siblings won't get with their dad—a lone tear escapes and runs down my cheek, which I catch with the sleeve of my jumper before anyone notices.

We are far from a traditional family. All five kids have only shared perhaps two weeks collectively together in our lifetimes, and we only have our father in common (except for the last two, who also share a mother). And yet, get us in a room together and we are undeniably related, plus lucky enough to get along like a house on fire. With the eldest overseas and the three youngest deeply engrossed in their own lives (as they should be, at their ages), the person left to care for Dad is me. I choose it, but I also know there's no one else to do it. It's me or bust. And I have a habit of both pushing myself too hard and struggling to accept help from others—both of which follow me into my role as Next of Kin.

There is no perfect family dynamic or care team when someone you love is terminally or chronically ill, or living with a disability. Everyone muddles through, doing the best they can. Sometimes, and in some instances often, someone's best is not the same as your best. You can spend precious time lamenting their lack of support or apparent interest in care, or you can accept that everyone gives what they're able to give and it's almost never equal. You're each bringing to the table your life experiences, beliefs, values, relationship to and history with that person, as well as your bandwidth and capacity at that point in time—physically and emotionally. Care, loss and grief are fertile grounds for resentment and estrangement in families, but they're also rich soils for growth and connection. I'm including this because I can't tell you how many conversations I have had with people who carry angst towards family members who do less, or who meddle too much, or who don't show up in the ways they are (or the ways they'd like them to).

There are a few principles that helped me here:

- **Assume everyone is doing their best.** Most people are, most of the time, doing their very best. If they don't show up, maybe they can't. You can be disappointed and you can be upset, but do your best to let them off the hook so you aren't carrying bad juju around. Ask yourself: 'What's the most generous interpretation of their situation?'

- **Know you can't do it for them.** You can lead a horse to water, but you can't make it drink. How people behave is something they have to live with on the other side of this experience, so acceptance is your best friend here. You can gently encourage, but let people move at their own pace. If that pace is a standstill, that's all they can manage at this point in time. You can twist yourself into as many knots as you like about it, but that won't spur them into action—it'll just make you look and feel like a pretzel.

- **Remember that money makes people do strange things.** We'll dive into this more in Part 3, but it's worth acknowledging that where money is involved, or precious belongings, people can get grabby. This wasn't my experience; my family were patient and generous and kind as I sorted out Dad's affairs, but I've heard from many people who haven't been as lucky. And, from what I hear, the more there is at stake, the grabbier people can get.

- **Rest in the fact that the universe is watching.** Act with as much integrity as you can muster in how you behave and how you treat people, because just as they have to live with how they behave, you do too. Ask yourself: 'How would my highest self behave here?'

Our team consisted of—to varying degrees—Dad's kids, his 90-year-old mother, his sister, his son-in-law, our doula and, when they were together, his girlfriend. Care teams take on myriad forms: sometimes it's a motley crew like ours or a more traditional family setup, and other times it's a chosen family of friends. Sometimes, for one reason or another, there's very few people around to care for someone, and other times there's no one. If I had a dollar for every time one of the nurses visiting Dad said they see people on their own all day every day, I'd be a Kardashian. Probably the poorest Kardashian, but still. Deciding on who will care and who will help (both personally and professionally) is worthy of dedicating some time and thought to, because when things go wrong, you'll need all hands on deck.

In developing countries, there is often no choice but for families to take on the brunt of care. In developed countries, we have a tendency to outsource care and there is more choice to do so, but those choices aren't available to all. However, the vast majority of the planet isn't in a position to throw unlimited resources at caring for someone they love, and most people have to provide care while also navigating the relentless demands of their already full lives. So, we work with what we have.

Figure 5.1 shows a macro view.

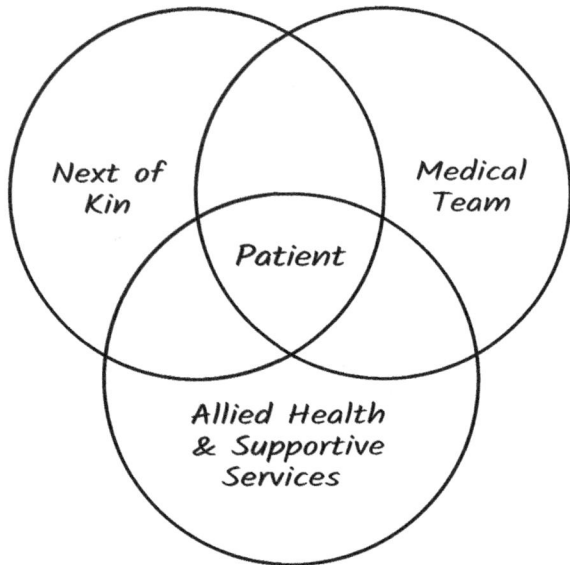

Figure 5.1 Your care team

Your professional care team might include people like:

- A general practitioner (GP) or family doctor
- Nurses
- Specialist(s) (like an oncologist, psychiatrist or surgeon)
- Counsellor or psychologist
- Social worker
- Spiritual care practitioner (like a rabbi, priest or even a doula)
- Allied health professional(s) (like a physiotherapist, occupational therapist or pharmacist).

Care truly is a team sport, and while it's very likely you're the captain, you'll be heavily reliant on the rest of the team to deliver great care.

Generation sandwich

All around the world, every day of the week, people are trying to care for the people they love while working and parenting and trying to maintain friendships, doing some exercise, staying across current affairs, paying their bills and not drowning in their own lives. Their dreams, goals and basic needs are carefully placed on a shelf to gather dust because there simply is no room left for them once all the doing is done. They end the day with more on their to-do list than when the day began, and no one knows this better than the sandwich generation.

Whoever coined that term has clearly never been in the position it was intended to describe — caring for young children and ageing parents at the same time. Two completely different sets of needs, with someone — usually a woman — at the centre feeling like one of those Mr Stretch dolls from the 1980s whose overly toned arms stretch way beyond their natural capacity. Working parenthood feels impossible as it is; adding in the additional layers of logistical and emotional complexity that come with caring for someone you love who is ill, injured or simply ageing is enough to tip anyone over the edge. And yet, day-in, day-out, we do it. We're the first generation to do so, but as we continue to live longer and have babies later, this experience will become very much the norm.

I wish I had some magical advice here that would make this challenge easier. I don't. The best I've got is to acknowledge that it's unbelievably hard and you're going to drop balls left, right and completely off the court. What I do know is that our generation is also the first to understand—and champion—the power of repair with our children. I know this first-hand. It took many months after Dad died for me to de-wobble my wobbly kids. My eldest in particular had acutely felt my absence, which had exacerbated her anxiety and affected her sleep, learning and confidence. I could see it happening: I did everything in my power to offset it, and I have worked hard to repair it ever since. I'm telling you this because when we try to 'do it all', there is always, always a cost. We can't rely on repair, but sometimes it's the best we can do.

While everyone's time is finite, and without having a crystal ball, I knew while I was caring for Dad that his time was probably more finite than mine and my children's. What I was doing wasn't forever—it was just for now. I have an incredible husband, who took a step back at work to be more available for our girls while I was caring for Dad. My mum stepped up to help big time, even though her relationship with Dad had been strained at best. My friends took my kids for play dates and their teachers held them when I couldn't. Little kids have a fairly shallow concept of time, but I assured mine frequently that life wouldn't be like this forever. I involved them in Dad's care, often taking one at a time for sleepovers at Papa's until the risk of them seeing something scary became too great. They held his hand, cheered him up and brought some light to the dark backdrop of our lives.

I was lucky to live a 10-minute drive from Dad's apartment. I was even luckier to have an incredible support network, the ability to survive on only my husband's wage, and work I could scale back and still be paid well for when I *was* able to dip my toe in without losing a job I needed to survive. It's not lost on me that this isn't the experience of the vast majority of carers, and I am in full support of the fact that we need to create policies to better support them.

Until that day, here's a few things that helped me.

- **Tell your family and friends you need their help.** Don't wait for them to offer, because when people don't know what to do they tend to do nothing. Can they pick up your kids one day a week and keep them until you can get home? Make a meal for your freezer? Pick up your medications from the pharmacy? Don't be a martyr and try to do it all yourself. You've survived this far in the big, bad world; you can sit in the discomfort of saying four words: I. Need. Your. Help.

- **Tell work what's going on.** Every industry and workplace is different, but I don't subscribe to the notion of keeping work and home separate. Let's face it, even if we were still trying to, that pesky virus that shook the world by its tonsils completely obliterated any barrier that was left. If your care responsibilities are likely to impact your work, which they probably will, find the most empathic boss in your workplace and tell them what's going on. You might not even be asking for anything yet, just their understanding if you're not quite yourself. Their response might surprise you.

- **Speak to your kids' teachers.** If you have school-aged children, tell their teachers what's happening at home. Kids take everything on and feed off your energy. If you're (understandably) absent, stressed or upset, that lands on them, whether they show signs of it at home or not. If their teachers know, they can provide an additional layer of support and help compensate in the schoolyard and classroom.

- **If you have a partner, tell them what you need.** I must've been a saint in a previous lifetime, because I got to marry one in this one. The way he stepped up to care for me, our children and my dad in our time of need was nothing short of heroic. He asked frequently what I needed, and anticipated those needs as much as he could. He didn't once complain, even when he absolutely could've and probably really wanted to. But partners are not mind readers, no matter how well they know you. Tell them what you need. Monthly, weekly, daily, hourly if you have to. And remember—they have needs too. Their giving is not an endless tap, just as yours isn't, so they'll need to top up the coffers at some stage as well.

You'll notice these all require you to communicate with people about what's going on. I know some people hold their cards (very) close to their chest, and all I can say is that when you are Next of Kin, it's not the time to be private—it's time to be human. If people don't know, they can't support you. And you need their support, even if you've traditionally not been very good at asking for it. If things get exponentially harder, you'll be glad to already have some support and understanding in place.

Leaning on each other isn't just vital to our survival, it's what makes us thrive. In their book *The Good Life: Lessons from the World's Longest Scientific Study of Happiness*, co-authors and directors of the Harvard Study of Adult Development, Robert Waldinger and Marc Schulz, write:

> ... human beings are social creatures; in essence this simply means that each of us as individuals cannot provide everything we need for ourselves. We can't confide in ourselves, romance ourselves, mentor ourselves or help ourselves move a sofa. We need others to interact with and to help us, and we flourish when we provide that same connection and support to others. This process of giving and receiving is the foundation of a meaningful life.

I couldn't agree more, yet I am about to learn what happens when you give too much.

CHAPTER 6

Harriet Potter, the stone and the buoy

Dad's final weeks take everything I have left to give. I've been white-knuckling through for months now and while I have waved the white flag a number of times, the responsibility of Dad's care has firmly — and willingly — remained with me. One particularly tough night, on not enough sleep and a steady diet of anxiety and Maltesers, I faint at 4 am and smack my face on the metal hospital bed we've had delivered to the house, splitting my forehead and lip and almost breaking my nose. I spend the morning in the emergency department and come back with a glued-up face and a battle scar to rival Harry Potter — a perfect lightning symbol on my forehead. Luckily Dad was oblivious to the entire ordeal, in the haze of what was to be his final day on Earth. But I am left with a lifelong reminder of what happens when you push yourself too far, forever wearing the toll of care on my face.

You're probably familiar with the term 'burnout', used to describe a state of physical, mental and emotional exhaustion. It has historically been attached to our professional lives — an occupational hazard typically reserved for the wealthy, because low-income workers don't have the luxury of a term like burnout. But carers also experience burnout, which is understandable given you're layering someone else's needs over the top of your own and — in many cases — over the top of people you're already caring for.

Burnout feels like your candle has run out of wick; you don't have what you need to continue to function, let alone shine. But *your* health and wellbeing matter just as much as the person you're caring for, arguably more so given that if you burn out, there may not be anyone else to care for them.

Signs of burnout are similar to those for severe stress or depression. They might include:

- Physical and/or emotional exhaustion
- Withdrawing from family and friends or losing interest in activities you once enjoyed
- Feeling helpless or hopeless, or overwhelmingly irritable, frustrated or angry towards other people
- Changes in appetite and/or weight
- Changes in sleep patterns
- Inability to concentrate
- Getting sick more often.

Looking back, I can see just how burned out I was. I ticked every box on the list and wore my exhaustion like a badge (or something more subtle, like a sticker perhaps) of honour. It was a sign of just how committed I was to the cause, and I figured I could sleep when I was dead. Which is ironic because, by the end of our journey, that's pretty much how I felt. But on the way, even when I was sleep-deprived, pre-emptively grieving or under the weather, I was also lit up with purpose. Alive, on task, almost on fire with purposeful *doing*. I was making a difference to Dad's one precious life, and the pain of losing him felt like it could be somewhat offset by the fact that if he was going to die, I was going to give him the best death in the history of deaths. Or at least in the top three.

This is the dilemma of care: it can feel impactful and exhausting and vital and impossible all at once. Most people who aren't caring for another struggle to practise self-care, so how are you supposed to fit it in when a huge proportion of your time is spent caring for someone else? Well, you embed some healthy micro-habits, around the same themes we all know make a difference when it comes to our health. I like to think about it like this: *What's the **minimum viable intervention** that will help me feel a tiny bit better **today**?*

For example:

- If you can't find the time to **exercise,** can you walk around the block? Go up and down the stairs twice? Do five minutes of yoga?
- If you can't **eat well,** can you cut out one thing that's not helping or add in one thing that will? Cut your evening wine perhaps, or your afternoon raid of the biscuit tin—just for today. Add in something green at dinner, or drink a big glass of water. What's *one tiny thing* you could do to nourish your body?
- If you can't **see your friends,** can you call one of them for a 10-minute chat over the phone? Can someone come over to care *with* you for 30 minutes?
- If you can't **get eight hours' sleep,** can someone take over so you can stick in your earplugs, put your phone on silent and top up your reserves with an afternoon nap? A nap is a game changer when you're depleted.
- If you can't **get professional psychological support or therapy,** do you have a good general practitioner (GP) or skilled friend you could download to? Sometimes, when we're overwhelmed, we just need to talk it out—and we need to carve out space to do that.

The stone or the buoy

We all have (and need) coping mechanisms. Life is stormy, and sometimes there are things that require coping with. Some coping mechanisms are good for us while some are not, and it's worth being aware of what behaviours we tend to lean on when we're under pressure. Some of us eat. Some drink or take drugs. Some have sex with strangers. Some work out relentlessly. Some work to excess. Some doomscroll on social media. Some spend money they don't have on things they don't need. I'm no stranger to any of those, and reading through that list you might find you're familiar with some too.

If you've ever done swimming lessons or any kind of water safety training, you might remember being told that people who are drowning can panic and scramble onto the closest thing to them. If the closest thing to them is another person, sadly what can happen is that the other person drowns in the process. Care can feel like you're in the middle of the ocean on a choppy day, and the person you're caring for is panicking. Even the strongest swimmers get caught out here and can find themselves quickly being dragged under. And if no one's coming to save us, we're going to need to save ourselves.

If we stick with this analogy, I like to think of coping mechanisms as either a stone or a buoy. Imagine you're in water so deep you're not able to stand. If someone threw you a stone, you'd sink. If they threw you a buoy, you'd float for long enough to figure out how to get back to shore.

Let's take a look at both.

Stones weigh us down. They might make us feel good in the moment, but they have a cost—physically, mentally, emotionally, spiritually or financially. These are often things we take in or act out. We might take in alcohol, drugs or too much comfort food. We might act out by overspending, gambling, procrastinating on social media, engaging with people who aren't good for us in ways that aren't good for us, or doing things that aren't good for us—working too much, working out too much, trying to control everything and everyone around us (guilty).

Buoys, on the other hand, lift us up. They're not very exciting, and like a buoy made from foam and rope, they're usually the same old things that have kept us afloat forever. Moving our bodies. Talking with friends. Eating fresh, healthy foods. Managing our stress by reading a book. Getting some sleep. Doing the work to maintain connection and community even when our social life feels non-existent. Paying our bills, even though we really don't want to. Going out for dinner with our partner or a friend, even when we're tired and would rather hit the couch (again). While these mundane things feel less important in times of stress, they are vital to our wellbeing and our survival.

Let me tell you about one of my favourite stones. If you've read my work, scrolled my Instagram or crossed paths with me in the last 20+ years, you might know alcohol and I have had a long and complicated love affair. When I was young it made me act dumb but feel cool, and as I got older my trusty crutch matured with me, elevating from Passion Pop and Goon of Fortune to $30 bottles of Shiraz and the occasional bottle of French when I was feeling fancy.

Outside of my family, alcohol had been one of my longest-standing relationships: cheap (bar the French), accessible and always, always there for me. We'd broken up before, many times, once for an entire year. But like all good bad relationships, we always found a way back to each other. The clarity I felt in the off-seasons always outweighed the buzz (and bloat) of the boozy ones, but given the chance to sit with a good friend and a glass of wine for a little life debrief (one of the greatest pleasures), I couldn't say no. It was too juicy, too connective, too good for my soul. I mean, we couldn't catch up for a *lemonade*, right? We are adults! Adults that have earned the legal right to consume poison that slows down time, bypasses whatever comes before relaxation and opens us up like clams. So, when I was caring for Dad, you can bet your bottom dollar I was exercising that right. I was contending with two small children who believe sleep is for the weak, a career that is equal parts thrilling and infuriating, and an impossibly broken heart from nursing and knowing I would soon be losing my beloved dad. Making it through any day without falling apart felt worthy of a parade, or at the very least a glass of Pinot.

Dad and I shared a love for Campari—a bitter Italian spirit that weirdly tastes a bit like medicine but is delicious with some soda and a squeeze of fresh orange. Seeing him and the bottle made me feel relief—he was still here. And I was never going to miss the chance to say cheers to that. But as Dad got sicker, he slowly turned on our shared friend. First, he asked for them weaker. Then they were weaker and unfinished. Next, they were untouched. Then he stopped saying yes altogether and I knew our little ritual was over. Dad seemed as sad about it as I felt, and in solidarity I switched to lime cordial when we were together—our feeble attempt at making tap water more exciting. But away from Dad, I kept it up in his honour—making Campari and soda my drink of choice when out, and my go-to drink at home. I figured it was probably better for my waistline than beer, better for my teeth than red wine and, given it tasted like medicine, it was probably *good* for my mental health.

I stuck with my ritual after Dad died. I made it through my first Christmas, New Year and even my 40th birthday with a Campari in hand—a tiny, invisible thread of connection between me and him, wherever he was. But after a while it just didn't hit the same. I'd reached a different phase of bereavement and desperately needed to pour some of the care I'd been giving Dad back into myself, so I started questioning whether it was time to break up with booze. I took a dozen of my favourite girls out for oysters and more bottles of champagne than we could count, and then I decided to give it away for a while. I didn't put an end date on it; I didn't announce it to the world immediately. I just stopped. I'm now more than a year into sobriety and can hands-down say it is the best thing I ever did for myself. It's a cliché, but sobriety really is my superpower.

I share that because I know some stones actually feel like crutches—things you not only deserve but feel like you wouldn't survive without. You know best, and timing is everything—and making big lifestyle changes may not be possible or even smart when you are in the throes of caring for someone you love. It's okay to have things in your life that aren't perfect for your wellbeing, but my hope is that you know your health is as important as anyone else's. Our health is our most important asset; without it, everything else falls away.

Advice from a deathwalker

Deathwalkers or death doulas are people who walk the dying and their loved ones through the process of death. They might help with administrative tasks, put together a ceremony or visit a dying person at their bedside to talk about the spiritual side of death. I'll never forget interviewing deathwalker Zenith Virago—she's probably the foremost death educator in Australia—on how women, when caring for others, put themselves and their health at the bottom of their to-do lists…to their detriment.

'I bury women who don't listen,' she told me.

She's referring to women not listening to their own bodies, and if it sounds like she's being dramatic, she's not. Highly respected medical journal *The Lancet* published some quite famous research in 1995 by American clinical psychologist, Professor Janice Kiecolt-Glaser. She's the director of the Ohio State University Institute for Behavioral Medicine Research and focuses on something called psychoneuroimmunology—the study of the effect of the mind on health and disease. The study looked at women caring for a loved one with dementia, comparing them to similar women who weren't under that same stress. They gave both groups what is called a punch biopsy, which sounds more violent than it is. They removed a small piece of skin from just above their elbows, and watched to see how the wounds healed in order to understand how psychological stress impacts our bodies' ability to heal. While the study was small, the results had big implications—the carers' wounds took significantly longer to heal than the wounds of those who weren't carers—nine days longer, in fact.

Kiecolt-Glaser's subsequent work, and more like it, tells us that carers have poorer physical, mental and emotional health than comparable people who aren't in a position of caring for someone they love. Remember the concept of health debt we talked about back in Chapter 2? When the body, mind and heart is under fire, there are less resources (or savings) left with which to fight disease and keep people happy and healthy. This was true in my own life; I ran up Dad's stairs like my knee cartilage would last forever, ate ice cream with him every night (because why wouldn't I) and drank Campari sodas like they were the only liquid on offer. I don't regret any of it, but I couldn't have kept doing it for much longer. My body was falling apart and as much as we'd like our health to patiently wait its turn for our attention, it doesn't work like that. If we go too far into health debt, we pay the price. So, we need to ensure we don't borrow more energy than we can repay.

Sweet, sweet respite

Respite care is critical for carers. Having someone take over our care responsibilities, even for a few hours, can give us an opportunity to reset, gather ourselves and reinvigorate for what's to come. It's a chance to replenish when we are already digging too deep, before the debt collectors start knocking on our metaphorical door. Respite might be delivered at a residential care institution like a hospital or hospice, or it might be delivered at home or in the community. It might be delivered by family and friends or by a respite care provider. It might be overnight or for a weekend or even just for a few hours, but it is all designed to give you—the carer—a short-term break from the demands of care.

Whenever I had a moment for respite, I stupidly used it to catch up on the rest of my life. But I never made a dent in the piles of life admin that had been accumulating while I was living in Dad's parallel universe. I should have taken myself to the beach for a swim, done some sort of self-care practice or even just thrown a rug out at the park and lain down with a book. File that one under: 'Do as I say, not as I do.' Because the only antidote to burnout is finding ways to get some respite.

CHAPTER 7
Spoongate

Dad is trying to buck the system. All the literature and expert opinion says that by now he should have stopped eating, as his body shuts down in preparation for death. Not only has he not stopped eating, he's upped his game. He has first breakfast, then second breakfast. First breakfast is porridge at home: oats cooked in almond milk with some honey, then topped with toasted nuts and seeds with more honey, cold milk and a blob of butter, which allows him to take his morning medications and get ready for the day. By the time he's in 'the pocket', he's feeling good and wants to get out, or feeling anxious and wants to get out. We make our way slowly to one of the many cafés surrounding Dad's house for second breakfast, one of the perks of living in the middle of an urban town. Some days it's French toast, others pancakes and others again he'll mix it up with shakshuka. We drink coffee and talk and sometimes laugh, and it's like we're any other father and daughter having a breakfast date. It's time I am so, so grateful for. 'Second breakfast' becomes common vernacular between me and the doula, shared with a quiet, knowing smile as we jump through any hoop Dad places in our path. Second breakfast is a nice hoop.

Before long, second breakfast changes. We go from walking there to using a walking stick, then to pushing him in the wheelchair. We go from sitting through breakfast to having to take one then multiple breaks to go for little walks up and down the street, Dad's body desperately pushing out life-force energy that makes him want to move, and move immediately. We go from eating everything to doggy bags to emptying uneaten boxes of food from the fridge. Dad has been trying to override the body's natural inclination to stop eating because he knows that's what happens at the end—and he isn't ready for the end yet.

When someone who doesn't know the sacred porridge recipe attempts to make it for first breakfast and fails, Dad's disappointment is visceral. Even when told what to do, the maker brings their own experience to the breakfast table. There is porridge nuance: the rate at which you heat, the frequency and vigour with which you stir, the amount of honey or nuts you deem appropriate, the balance of hot and cold and, of course, the presentation. Our world had become so small that little things started feeling like the biggest things.

Dad asks if we can talk, and I get that sinking feeling I'm either about to get in trouble or be delivered bad news. Dad tells me he's struggling to understand some people's choice in spoons.

'Spoons?' I ask, internally questioning whether we are in fact talking about spoons or if Dad's cognitive decline has reached a new low.

'I just don't understand why anyone would give someone a soup spoon to eat breakfast with,' he explains, confirming we are indeed talking about actual spoons.

'Ha,' I offer a half-laugh that straddles supportive solidarity in case he's being serious, but also covers me if he bursts out laughing, which I am secretly hoping he does. Instead, he barrels on.

'It just shows no thought, no care, no consideration…' he rants, gesticulating weakly with his hands as though he's raving about a disliked politician or climate change.

I make a mental note to brief everyone that soup spoons should be strictly avoided at breakfast time and must only be used for their designated purpose of spooning soup. I listen, trying to convey appropriate concern and attention with my facial expressions so he feels seen and heard, before assuring him I'll tell everyone to be more spoon-aware.

Clearly, 'spoongate' wasn't really about the spoon but rather about control—controlling the little things because Dad couldn't control the biggest thing of all. If anyone else was fighting me on spoons, I'd tell them they needed to get a hobby. But Dad was dying, so Dad got to bitch about spoons. And I would pick my battles, allowing space for his disdain for ill-timed soup spoons so I could save my push-back tickets for harder, more critical issues.

During this time, life became a series of little deaths. The death of his ability to walk to breakfast. The death of his ability to finish breakfast. The death of his ability to want breakfast at all. A million little deaths, sometimes by lunch.

This movie sucks

Watching someone you love physically, mentally and emotionally decline in front of your eyes is like watching a terrible movie you can't turn off. Depending on the context, it's possible you'll notice little things changing, then perhaps bigger things. I suspect most of the time the person the changes are happening to notices as well, whether they let on or not.

Changes might be subtle or obvious, and may be due to a number of things:

- A symptom of their illness or injury
- A side effect of their treatment
- A simultaneous condition that may be related or unrelated to their illness or injury
- A symptom of, or reaction to, their situation.

Being around someone a lot can make the changes less noticeable, like when you have small children and it's only when you take them out of context you realise how much they've grown. Which is why keeping some simple notes is incredibly worthwhile, even if it's just getting into the habit of jotting something down each day or every few days.

You're essentially looking to capture any change, perhaps:

- An **improvement,** which could be due to the issue resolving or effective treatment
- A **deterioration,** which could be progression of illness or injury, poorly managed symptoms or something new altogether.

I was also interested in Dad's mood, and how the whole experience was landing on him. I was just the person accompanying him—I wasn't the one having the experience. So, I'd make notes on that too, as a record of when he was particularly moody or emotional or happy. This might sound a bit odd and clinical, but I think our lives are essentially one giant experiment. And experiments need data. In a terminal illness setting, I'd also extend my note-taking to things Dad said to me, jotting them down in quotation marks so I'd remember they were direct quotes. Hear me now, understand me later—you think you'll remember, but you won't. And having the exact words written down gives them a reliability that has allowed them to stick with me even as the sound of Dad's voice starts to feel further away in my mind.

You might remember back in Chapter 2 I talked about the body playing dominoes, especially when it comes to risk factors for poor health and chronic disease. When the body is shutting down, it's kind of the same thing. The body has a process it follows, a sheet of music only it can read. Depending on where the disease is, it will either slowly and systematically or rapidly and dramatically bring life to an end. For the observer, witnessing this process is heartbreaking. That's worth acknowledging because while we rarely talk about it, watching someone you love deteriorate, struggle or die is up there with the hardest things I think we go through as human beings.

The Harvard Study of Adult Development (that I mentioned back in Chapter 5) is one of my favourite scientific studies. Since 1938, it has been following what is a now significant number of people to try to understand what makes a good life. They started with 724 participants—two study groups of men in Boston. One group (268) were Harvard sophomores, and the other (456) were boys and young men from some of the poorest neighbourhoods in the Boston area. Only men of a certain privilege would be able to go to Harvard, so looking at only them would make any findings less applicable to a broader population. Having the other group as a control would give them something to compare the Harvard group to. They only included men because at that time, only men were allowed to go to Harvard. But in the years since they've expanded the study to include the wives and children of the original cohort—a second and third generation of study participants to broaden out the learnings.

Every few years, researchers collect the participants' health data, but they also sit down with them for in-depth interviews and ask them to complete questionnaires. They don't just ask them health questions, they ask about every facet of their lives—their relationships, work and feelings. While most healthcare studies capture a moment in time or rely on memory, this one captures the participants' experiences almost as they live them.

Having such deep and long-term data is a gift to our understanding of the human experience, and how it might be changing over time. I'm oversimplifying here, but one of the overarching learnings of the study is that our relationships are of vital importance to both our health and happiness, and the scientific evidence is clear that becoming a carer for the people we love when they are injured or ill can have a big impact on both.

'We know it's one of the most stressful experiences that people can have in their life when you have that responsibility,' Professor Marc Schulz, one of the directors of the study, tells me over Zoom from his home in Philadelphia.

'It's clear from lots of research that it [caring] affects our bodies in negative ways at multiple levels—stress hormones, inflammatory patterns, epigenetic patterns. It's pretty extraordinary how it gets into our bodies and affects us, and it's exhausting for most people as well. So this is a kind of profound experience.'

I tell Schulz caring for Dad was indeed one of the hardest but richest experiences of my life so far. He tells me that of the original study participants, 91 per cent served in World War II and describe their experiences there with similar language to that which carers use and that I used to describe caring for Dad, which seems fitting given that care can feel like warfare on your wellbeing, not to mention your soul.

'Their descriptions of their experience are incredibly kind of similar to what you just described, [but it's a] very different experience, right?' he shares with me. 'They talk about this [war] as the most harrowing and scary experience of their lives. In many ways, it was the worst experience of their lives, but they also talk about it with reverence.'

Schulz goes on to explain that there are three key parts to that reverence. The first is that they had a clear sense of purpose that felt unique in their lives — pure and compelling. Secondly, it was a mission they believed in, and finally it involved working closely with — and trusting — other people. They were in the foxholes together, so they literally had to have each other's backs.

These three key parts are alarmingly similar to the experience of caring for someone you love who is chronically or terminally ill. It *does* feel compelling and purposeful. It *does* feel like a mission you believe in. And you *do* form very intense and close relationships with the person you are caring for and the people you're caring alongside because you feel like you are fighting a war together. I of course don't know what it's like to go to war, but I do know what it's like to *feel* like you're in one. Schulz is right — it's exhausting. And the only thing that gets us through it is our people.

The love drug

When American neuroscientist and professor of psychology James Coan was studying post-traumatic stress disorder (PTSD), he was scanning brains using an MRI machine to try to better understand what was going on for people with PTSD and hopefully inform how new treatments were developed. One of the study participants was a man who was so affected by his intense combat experience in the Vietnam war he was unable to enter the MRI room without his wife with him. Coan made an exception and allowed the wife to come in, and when the noisy MRI machine started up and he became agitated, she instinctively held his hand. Coan could see that the simple act of his wife taking her distressed husband's hand in hers calmed him to the point where he was able to continue.

Intrigued, Coan developed a new study to see if he could find evidence for what had happened. He put a new set of study participants through a functional MRI machine, which allows researchers to see which parts of the brain are active when you apply a stimulus like having them perform a task. He showed participants one of two slides: a red slide meant there was a 20 per cent chance they would receive a small electrical shock, and a blue slide meant there was no chance they'd receive a shock.

Study participants were split into three groups:

- Group 1 had no one in the room with them
- Group 2 held the hand of a stranger
- Group 3 held the hand of their spouse.

The results were clear: the group who held the hand of their spouse had reduced anxiety and were calmer in the fear centres of their brains. But remarkably, they also experienced less pain if they *did* receive a shock, prompting the researchers to suggest that holding their spouse's hand appeared to have the same effect as a mild anaesthetic. Holding a stranger's hand helped, but not as much as holding the hand of a partner, and the better their relationship was, the stronger the effect. Which is a long way of saying that supporting someone you love through an illness or injury isn't just kind, it's medicine.

Dad and I were avid hand-holders, individually and together. His hands remained so much bigger than mine, even when I was fully grown. He had held mine while I was growing up, so to have the opportunity to hold his through his illness and darkest days—while he was growing *down*—was an honour and privilege I'll never forget. But it did also wreak havoc on my physical, mental and emotional health, and I don't feel like that's talked about enough, so I want to acknowledge it here.

The physical side of caring—especially when someone is critically injured, disabled or severely ill—is not to be sneezed at. Your neck will go, your back will go and your knees will be quick to remind you that physiotherapists exist for a reason. Getting the right equipment, support and techniques to move, bathe and care for them is paramount to your physical survival if they are unable or less able to care for themselves.

Consider if they might need:

- An electronic chair to stand up and sit down
- A chair or rail for the shower
- A commode on wheels over the toilet
- A wheelchair for longer distances
- An alarm they can press if they fall
- An electric bed to help them sit up
- A portable oxygen tank
- A jar-opener for when they lose grip strength
- Different pillows or bedding
- A fan or heater
- Incontinence pads
- A bell to get someone's attention.

Also, make sure you're really clear on exactly how to use everything. What training might you (and/or they) need to use that equipment? Get whoever supplies it to show you how to use it, and then show you again. Take notes, because it may not (and should not) always be you operating it. Ask if there's an instructional video you can fall back on if you forget, or a number you can call if you're unsure. Don't assume you'll 'work it out'. If you add any sort of emotion or stress into the mix, you don't want to get caught out fighting a disobedient wheelchair or injuring yourself because you instinctively tried to lift your person after a fall.

Get clear on what you'd do in an emergency. It's easy to think you'd just call an ambulance, and if the situation called for it you would. But someone already grappling with a severe illness or injury might not want to spend a night in the emergency department. Is there a helpline you can call for support at home? We had one through our hospice at home program that meant we could get a nurse to Dad's apartment within a few hours 24/7; depending on your situation and location, you might have something like that available to you too. Failing that, we also had printed action plans I or our doula would write up describing exactly what to do if Dad was feeling breathless and panicked, for example — both of which were hallmarks of his disease. It meant that if anyone else was there with him, both he and they had some level of comfort that they could support him through an attack by following a set of instructions stuck to the fridge so they couldn't get lost.

Get clear on what to do when things go wrong, before they do. Ask your doctors and yourself:

- What could go wrong here?
- What would our options be if that was to occur?
- Of those options, what would we choose to do in an ideal world?

That will inform the answers to questions like:

- If they fall and I'm the only one at home with them, what will I do? Do I call an ambulance so the paramedics can help me get them up? Do I call a friend and learn how we would get them up together?
- Is the person I'm caring for happy to go to a hospital if necessary or are they hell-bent on staying home?

- If they were to need a life-saving intervention like CPR (cardiopulmonary resuscitation), do they want to be resuscitated? (I go into this further in Chapter 10.)

There's a lot of 'figure it out as you go' in care, but the more you know about what your person would want in any given situation, the more effective you'll be at making decisions quickly when you need to. And this applies no matter who you're caring for. Take the example of a neurodivergent or anxious child who struggles with school drop-off. What could go wrong? And what could you do if that does occur? Your plan might fall apart, but you'll feel better if you have one to fall back on. Care is a partnership between you and the person you're caring for, supported by a whole bunch of others. You are in the foxholes together, but they are the one with their life on the line. We are just the lookout, watching every gut-wrenching moment from our position of relative safety. And at some point, they are going to have to get out of the foxhole and fight without us.

And yet, Dad doesn't want to die so he pushes on, determined to outlive the death sentences continually handed to him. And push on he does, with more time where we get to talk, think and be together. It's precious and painful and beautiful and awful and monumental and mundane all at once. And then, even with two-and-a-half years to 'prepare', the end nears, and I am, in no way, prepared.

CHAPTER 8
Deadlines

Dad and I are walking the long hospice hallway, hand in hand. We get to the end and bump into Pablo and Lucia. Pablo and Lucia are a giant stuffed donkey and camel, respectively, who have taken up residence in the hospice. They'd probably be more at home in a children's hospice, but they seem to quite like it here. We pat them, talk to them and ask how they are. It's absurd—but so is the fact we're in this place. This situation. So, we pat. Lucia has thick, black eyelashes stitched into her fur, but one side has come away and she's looking worse for wear, like she has had a big night and done a less-than-stellar job of washing her makeup off. Dad suggests we drive to the shops to get her a new set of lashes and we giggle like schoolgirls as we plan our top-secret mission.

We secure the lashes and come straight back, figuring poor Lucia can't live another minute with sub-par lashes. We glue them on and realise we've made her look worse—part forgotten toy and part hungover drag queen. We admit defeat and make a mental note to ask my nan to bring her sewing kit next time so Lucia can be upgraded to the lashes she deserves. Lucia looks ridiculous, but Dad and I get some decent mileage out of how funny we think we are. It's a side effect of our relationship; our humour is dark but we can always find the light, even in the bleakest of times.

I've been an adult for many years at this stage, but now I can feel the pendulum swinging the other way in our dynamic. I have taken on the role of parent while he reverts to child. I know this is in some ways uncomfortable for him, and I make space for that discomfort amid the necessity the situation is calling for—encouraging independence wherever I can or whenever he seems to need it. Just like parenting, my job is to keep him fed, clean and as physically and emotionally comfortable as possible. But just like you can't prevent a child from falling over and scraping their knee, you can't prevent someone you love from going through what an ill or injured body is determined to go through, nor the daily grievances that come with that. No one can outrun the body they're in, and even the wealthiest of us can't buy our way out of a sick one.

It's at this point in the care journey that you have to start balancing their comfort with your sanity and survival. I knew Dad wanted to come home from hospice, but as a family we simply weren't equipped to support him appropriately at home. Dad's care needs had increased while he was in hospice, as his disease progressed and the breeze picked up on the edge of the cliff. I wanted more than anything to give him what he wanted, but there simply wasn't enough of me to go around— I was trying to care for my dying dad as well as parent two small children, and those two things just don't mix. Having someone at home with him most of the time wasn't going to cut it anymore—he needed support 24/7. The other people in our care team were giving what they could, and after several tough conversations I knew I wasn't going to be able to get any more out of them. My younger siblings had also started to worry about what they would do if something went wrong on their watch, scar tissue they didn't want to (and shouldn't have to) live with.

While I could do the bulk of Dad's care, I couldn't be there all the time and also couldn't live with the worry of something going wrong when I wasn't. I looked into private nurses who were going to cost thousands of dollars a week, but when I pitched it to Dad he seemed disappointed and almost offended by the suggestion. Supporting me through the process was our doula, who said she would step up and help me get Dad through what we anticipated would be his last weeks. Dad had been on his 'last weeks' for a year now, but with some respite under my belt while Dad was in hospice, I had gathered myself enough to know I could get through them, especially with increased support from our angel-on-earth doula.

When we knew he was coming home, we used our final hospice days to set up his apartment to better accommodate him. I worked with our hospice and aged care provider to get a hospital bed delivered to his home for his comfort, and pulled favours from Dad's friends to help dismantle and move the old bed out of the way. If I wasn't good at delegating before, I was an Olympic-level delegator by the time he came home.

Where you care for someone depends on a huge range of factors: their age, their diagnosis, what support you have at home, how much money you have to throw at it, how capable you feel and how comfortable they are. Some people find comfort in being in a facility where they can push a button and get medical attention, and others love nothing more than being able to be in their own home—and they're willing to risk less immediate care should they need it in order to be there. These are big themes: safety, dignity, capacity. What they have in common though is people at their core—both the person being cared for and the person (or people) providing the care. There is no 'right' answer, only the answer that is right for you. What I can say is that you are more capable than you will ever know, and I am eternally proud that we were able to—outside of his two weeks in hospice—care for and allow Dad to die at home, as was his wish.

With time running out, I knew it was important for me to also have some time with Dad as his daughter, not as his carer or Drill Sergeant Casey. I needed to just *be* with him. But *being* is not my strong suit. I'm much more comfortable in the realm of *doing*—a thinly veiled attempt at outrunning my emotions that I'm sure is also the reason I have to be doing at least three other things while watching TV. But if I have one regret in the final weeks, it's that I didn't stop to just *be* more often. Sure, I read to him and brushed his hair and rubbed his swollen feet, but I never stopped to sit in the gravity of what was happening. I couldn't. We'd come too far for me to fall apart now. And Dad had started pushing me away, as we all tend to do when life isn't going our way, taking out our deepest frustrations on the people closest to us.

I was trying to manage Dad's death like it was the biggest, most important project I would ever deliver. And instead of feeling supported, in his worst moments he simply felt like I was rushing him towards the last scene, even though I'd given up the last few years of my life and moved my young family across the country in an attempt to give him the opposite—as much time as humanly possible. I suppose he was starting to feel like a burden, and I was learning quickly that no matter how hard I tried, life had served up a sh*t sandwich, and Dad was the one who had to eat it.

Voluntary assisted dying

Much earlier in the journey, Dad had willingly signed up for voluntary assisted dying (VAD). He told me he was grateful to live and die in a time where that was available to him—a 'get out of jail free' card that would allow him some control over how he was to bow out of his own life.

VAD enables a patient to legally access medication that will cause their death. They can choose to take the substance themselves or have it administered to them by a trained medical practitioner. The pathway to approval was relatively straightforward, albeit cumbersome and with necessary safeguards; it's understandably not as simple as having a general practitioner (GP) write a script. Dad allowed me to be his sounding board throughout the process, but he quietly booked and attended those appointments on his own.

All states have their own process, but to be eligible in Western Australia (and these are similar across the country), the dying person has to:

- Be 18 years of age or older
- Be an Australian citizen or permanent resident, and have been generally residing in the state for at least 12 months
- Be diagnosed with at least one disease, illness or medical condition that is advanced, progressive and likely to cause death within six months or, in the case of a neurodegenerative disease (such as Parkinson's or motor neurone disease), within 12 months
- Be suffering or expected to suffer in a way that cannot be relieved in a manner the person considers tolerable
- Have decision-making capacity and be acting voluntarily and without coercion.

It's worth noting that at the time of writing, VAD is still illegal in the Northern Territory and will only become available in the Australian Capital Territory from November 2025. VAD is available in New Zealand, as well as in some US jurisdictions. The UK parliament backed a bill to pass VAD laws in late 2024, but it will take time to become available.

In Australia, the process differs between states. In Western Australia the person must be assessed by at least two doctors who are eligible and trained. The dying person makes a first request, followed by an assessment and written declaration, before making their final request and having the medication prescribed and dispensed. Dad wasn't sure how to position his potential use of VAD to his younger children, and while he had mentioned it to them briefly in the past, I think the resurrection of it being a possibility caught them off guard. Our doula had been recommended a recent episode of a TV show tackling the topic of VAD, and after watching it to determine its suitability, Dad suggested we use it as a tool to get my siblings across the idea. We gathered together to watch it, creating a space in which they could ask questions. I don't know if it ignited the discussion Dad wanted, but I do think it gave his younger children an opportunity to learn about it together, and showed them that the door was always open if they had questions or concerns.

I don't remember exactly what prompted Dad to make the final request. I just remember the doula and I starting to get concerned about his capacity to swallow. Because if you choose to self-administer, which is what Dad had chosen, you have to be able to mix and consume the liquid independently—no one can help you. Dad said he would get comfort in knowing the medication was in the house in case he decided on any given Tuesday he wanted out, so he made the final request and the state pharmacy—which dispenses the medication—set up a time to bring it to Dad's apartment and walk us through how to use it.

A week or so later, two women arrived at Dad's apartment with two identical red toolboxes, as though they had come to fix the sink. We sat at the dining table, making small talk as if we were about to share fondue rather than talk about the substance that would kill my dad. They were kind and calm, and I wondered how they felt about this part of their job. They explained that the two red boxes they'd brought with them were a replica of the real kit, and the real thing. They said that in order for them to leave the real kit with us, they needed to see that Dad was capable of mixing and consuming the liquid. And if he wasn't, they legally couldn't leave the kit in his possession.

Can we just pause here for a moment to acknowledge how bizarre this situation is? No one prepares you for the fact that there is a rehearsal for someone ending their life. Not just a 'here's how it works' instructional chat, but the dying person has to physically act out the process—including drinking the same amount of liquid—in front of a live audience. Dad passed the world's strangest test, and understandably retired to the couch to lay down. He was generally getting sleepier at this stage, often nodding off mid-conversation. I gave the women a teary, knowing look—one that was intended to say *thank you for being here, I know this is weird, sorry he's sleepy and I think we may have missed the boat on this whole thing,* but without words. I signed the paperwork and said goodbye to the women, and at Dad's request placed the locked death-box up high in his wardrobe, well out of the way of tiny fingers no matter how high they climbed or jumped. Then, we parked the whole thing.

One of the biggest challenges of advocacy at this late stage is that you may have competing variables. Dad had been abundantly clear that he wanted to go out on his own terms, 'with all his faculties' and 'very much awake'. As his swallow reflex started to wane, which it does at the end of life, he started to cough every time he drank anything—a simple sip of water could ignite a coughing fit. A coughing fit is one thing when it is with water, but another thing entirely when you're drinking a substance that will end your life. Wanting to uphold his wishes, the doula and I gently asked whether he felt the need to set a date to use the VAD kit—a literal deadline—before that window of opportunity closed. Dad was understandably resistant; I wouldn't want to set a date for my death either. Sitting down with him to lay out the fact that I was concerned he wouldn't get what he wanted was one of the hardest and most emotionally challenging conversations of my life.

Because what I was inherently saying was that he looked like he was getting worse—and that was the last thing my dad wanted to hear.

Even though VAD was what he wanted in theory, he couldn't bring himself to use it. When he did reluctantly set a date, his doctor told him she didn't think he'd make it. At this stage, we switched to practitioner-administered, where a trained doctor or nurse practitioner would come to Dad's apartment and inject him with the substance instead. The thinking was that this would give him more flexibility on time, regardless of his swallow reflex. I called the nurse practitioner to gauge her availability so I could feed any information back to Dad. I knew there weren't many practitioners trained to deliver VAD, and I wanted Dad to know how much flexibility he had on timing. As soon as she answered the phone, her casual tone conveyed no warmth, no recognition of what I was calling to talk about. She almost seemed annoyed at my intelligence-gathering exercise, huffily giving me days and times she was available and running me through her schedule as though I was booking in a haircut. I hoped that if this was the way Dad went, it wasn't with her.

We all hold personal beliefs around death, and it was mine that people should be able to die in the way they choose. I have heard of families having beautiful experiences with VAD, but in all honesty the thought of gathering to watch Dad end his life was more than my heart could take. I'd have made my heart take it because it's what he wanted, but I'd be lying if I said I wasn't freaked out by it. No matter how nice we made the room, what music we played or how okay we all were with the idea, the thought of having a day and time in the diary for Dad to die put my anxiety on steroids. It didn't feel right when I played it out like a movie in my mind. I couldn't *see* it, and I can make myself see pretty much anything. It turned out, I didn't need to. Dad would never use VAD. The universe did what it does and took matters into its own hands, and I think honestly Dad was relieved. I know I was. Dad's death played out exactly as it should have, on his own time and at his own pace, with many of the people he loved most in the room.

PART III

Legal and Financial Care

Having difficult conversations, planning ahead to avoid legal headaches and dealing with the costs of care — of which there are many.

Before we get started on the minefield that is law, love and money, please note that—like the rest of this book—nothing here can constitute advice. If you need guidance on crafting some dance moves for a party or my top picks when it comes to chips from the supermarket, I can advise on that. But for legal and financial advice, you need a professional who understands your unique situation and can advise accordingly.

CHAPTER 9

Hats

Having hard conversations is kind of like wearing a sun hat with a neck flap. There's nothing cool or fun about it, and you feel like a bit of a wally wearing it, but it's absolutely necessary for protecting you from the scorching sun. It's about preventing future pain, even if it's uncomfortable to wear in the moment.

Getting our affairs in order is like writing a love letter to the people we love most. It requires some worst-case scenario thinking, so if you prefer to live with your head in the clouds, I'm going to need you to plant your feet firmly on the ground for a little while. Don't worry, you can head back up there when we're done. Also, how *is it* up there? I've always wanted to know...

Dad is laying on the spare bed while I go through boxes of his things, holding them up like an auctioneer. He is at the phase of sorting called 'regret'. The question isn't 'Does this spark joy?' but 'Can this come with me in my coffin?', to which the answer is almost always no. I watch his heart break when we get to things that hold no financial value but are priceless to him—a small clay animal one of his sons made when they were little, a feather he collected with one of his daughters, and a piece of coal his little sister gave him 50 years ago that he's carried around ever since.

Ringing out from the phone on the bed is upbeat hold music from his super fund, and I have a spreadsheet open on my laptop titled 'Dad important things'. When the super guy (as in, the guy from the super fund—I can't comment on whether or not he is a super guy) joins us on the line, Dad motions to me with his eyes that he doesn't have the energy to speak. I tell super guy we're calling to set up third-party authorisation on Dad's accounts as we've been told when the time comes for me to wrap up his affairs, having that in place will make my job easier. We give the required member numbers and passwords, and Dad confirms he isn't tied up in a basement being coerced into making the call. Before long, third-party authorisation is in place and we get off the phone, grateful to have ticked another job off the list but deflated by the fact we had to do the job in the first place.

We are packing Dad's things to move him from one apartment to another. The old and new apartments are just around the corner from each other and not dissimilar in size and style, but one is a walk-up with three sets of stairs to the top floor and the other has a lift to the first floor. The stairs have been getting harder for Dad, so we are pre-emptively moving him to ensure he doesn't get to a point where he can't access his apartment. We joke about rigging up a surfboard with a rope to haul him up, but when I think about it seriously—which is part of my job description as his primary carer—it really is the strangest variety of forecasting as I try to predict what his decline might look like and on what timeframe. Wait too long and I might not be able to find another apartment in time, but pull the trigger too soon and I risk spooking Dad, who isn't quite ready to accept just how bad his situation is.

As I pack, he apologises frequently for not doing more to help, and I tell him again and again that I'm happy doing a few boxes each day and we'll get there together. As moving day nears, it becomes clear Dad is in no position to pack, help or even supervise. It also becomes clear that one can collect a whole lot of sh*t over their lifetime. I marvel at the volume of stuff, knowing my garage is already housing many more of Dad's belongings and wondering how on earth we're going to move everything here from one apartment (hello, stairs) to the other.

My husband and I (as well as a few dear helpers) manage to move Dad's small mountain of things, then Dad himself, from his old apartment to his new one over the world's longest day. I accidentally leave a few things at his old place—not precious things, just house things. An excellent dustpan and brush fall prey to the moving gods, which makes Dad annoyed. Without guidance, I have carefully packed everything into labelled boxes and yet, for the first few weeks at the new place, Dad can't find certain things. This too makes Dad annoyed. Dad being annoyed makes me annoyed. While I know he is grateful for everything we do and have done for him, moments like this make my job feel thankless. I am dropping the ball on everything outside of Dad, so when I can't even do a good job of something Dad-related, it makes me feel like a giant, exhausted failure.

Caring for someone you love who is ill or injured requires two very different skill sets in operation at the same time. Much of care is soft, nurturing, emotional. It needs gooey energy. And so much of what comes with wrangling care is practical, get-it-done, tough stuff energy. In the same hour you can be holding your loved one's hand as they grapple with their situation (gooey), cooking their dinner and eating with them (gooey), while simultaneously making eight phone calls and fielding six more—most of which require you to coordinate, convince or chase down things you want or need (tough stuff). The frequent gear changes can give you whiplash, and very few people are naturally good at both gears.

You're essentially trying to wear two hats at the same time. One hat is the sun hat with a neck flap, practical, strategic and kind of ugly—it's not cute but it gets the job done. The other hat is soft and fluffy—it feels good on but holds little by way of practical hat-value. By now you're probably imagining me (or yourself) wearing two very different hats at once and realising how ridiculous we look, which is akin to how you will sometimes feel. To get around this, I took my hat analogy into this stage of our lives. When Dad and I were doing administrative, legal or financial work, I would mime putting a hat on and say, 'I'm putting on my executor hat, Dad,' which signalled to him I was thinking and acting practically or strategically. It was a segue for him and allowed me a moment to step into a more practical, less gooey energy when I had to. And when I needed to step out of Drill Sergeant Casey mode and just be his daughter, I said so. This helped him soften when he needed to and allowed me a few precious moments of just being a girl losing her dad. These gear changes are important, and impartiality isn't the goal. Rather, it's about being able to dial into whatever energy you need in any given day, hour or minute.

Hard hat for hard chat

When you enter a building site or demolition zone, you're strongly encouraged to put on a hard hat — presumably in case an anvil falls out of the sky and lands on your skull. It doesn't prevent the anvil from falling, but it tries to prevent it from doing damage if it *does* fall and land on you. Getting your affairs in order — while you're well — is kind of the same. You're not *expecting* the anvil, but you're protected if it falls. And that might require some hard chat.

Conversations about end of life are tricky but, they are necessary — vital — for all families. Nothing I tell you here will make these conversations comfortable or fun, so you will need to sit in the discomfort of raising and having them. I've had many conversations with people who say things like, 'We don't talk about death' or 'We don't talk about money in our family.' This might be because of their beliefs, or it might be because they are relying on their spouse or partner to survive them and manage their affairs if they are incapacitated or die. But here's what I can tell you from experience: wrapping up someone's affairs, even when you have all the relevant documentation and it's a relatively straightforward estate, is painful. It took me the better part of a year, amid my grief, to finalise Dad's affairs. No one talks about the fact that when someone is terminally ill, once they die a whole other chapter of work begins. It's like climbing a mountain and getting to the top, only to realise there's another, bigger mountain to climb — you just couldn't see it because it was behind the one you were climbing.

The conversation you need to have in your family will differ depending on your situation, but if you *do* need to ignite a tough conversation, here's how I'd do it:

- **Plan it, don't thrust it on them.** I'm yet to find an effective segue that takes you from 'pass the pepper' to 'let's talk about what happens when you die'. Plant the seed that you'd like to have the conversation and then set a dedicated time to do so in the coming days or weeks. That gives everyone time to think and wrap their heads around the idea before you come together.

- **Pick your timing and setting for the conversation.** Don't do it at the end of a workday when everyone is knackered, or when there are small children around who will naturally demand attention. If home doesn't feel right, find somewhere that does. A noisy café or restaurant might not be right either—you know best, but it's worth some thought.

- **Be transparent about your objective.** The goal here is to smooth the potentially rocky path ahead should anything happen in the future. Once end-of-life planning is in place, you can all get on with living forever and rest assured that everything you need to execute on someone's wishes is in place. Because the only thing harder than grief is having to deal with administrative headaches while grieving. This conversation is a favour to your future selves.

- **Acknowledge these conversations are uncomfortable.** Very few people go into conversations about end-of-life planning fizzing with excitement. Open the conversation by acknowledging that these topics can feel a bit heavy, and watch everyone's shoulders drop a little as they exhale. This is hard stuff, so call it what it is—there's camaraderie in that.

- **Understand that you can only encourage.** You can't force someone to face their mortality, whether they're ill, injured or in perfect health and whether they're 30 or 90. Their life—and death—is up to them. If they refuse to engage with the objective of making life easier for whoever has to deal with their affairs should anything happen to them, that's their choice and you have to respect it.

In Chapter 10, we'll walk through the documents you need in place and therefore what you might cover in the conversation you open. I don't want to labour the communication piece too much, but it's worth noting that people's approach to hard chat is as varied as the people themselves. There are people who have everything we'll talk about here (and probably more) locked and loaded, safely squared away with a lawyer, and everyone involved already knows exactly what to do in the event of their demise. We're trying to be more like them. Then, there are people who have bits and pieces done. They have a will, they just don't know where it is. They want a cremation, they just haven't captured that desire anywhere. They *did* tell Uncle Bill once after a few beers, so surely he'll remember. Then, there are the people who put everything hard on the 'I'll deal with that later' list, which they never get to. We're all guilty of having that list, so these chapters are designed to help you get some of the most important decisions and documents of all of our lifetimes out of our heads and into a place where the people who will need them can access them.

Nola Ries is a professor of law at the University of Technology Sydney. I ask her where people tend to get it wrong when it comes to planning for end-of-life care, legally and financially.

'There are three categories,' she shares with me. 'So, one is not doing it at all. Second, would be leaving it until a crisis arises, and then the planning is very reactive to a crisis and is unduly stressful for everybody involved. And then the third problem is people do it proactively, but they don't do it as well as they can.'

She goes on to explain that one example of this third category is using DIY documents.

'This could be because they're looking to save money, but it might cost more in the long run,' she tells me. 'They get a DIY will kit, or they download some documents from the internet and they think that they've made appropriate documents, but there could be things they have missed. It's really important to think carefully about who you are appointing into these really powerful roles, and then also making sure the documents are drafted really well.'

It's my belief that communication is everything, especially when it comes to planning for end-of-life care. Ries agrees.

'Communication is essential for the people you are appointing to make decisions for you while you are still alive,' she tells me. 'So your financial Enduring Power of Attorney, your Enduring Guardian or [Enduring] Medical Power of Attorney, it's really important to sit down and talk through your wishes so that when that person has to act in those really legally powerful, but also very stressful roles, they know that what they are doing is consistent with your values and preferences.'

Sadly, there's no magical administration fairy who can come and help. But there are some handy people who can advise you and point you in the right direction if you need guidance.

- An **accountant** can advise on your financial setup and position. This might include super, bank accounts, shares and whether you have to go through the probate process—a legal process that verifies a will's validity and allows the executor to manage the deceased's estate.

- A **lawyer** can help you draft a will if your family or assets are complicated or you don't trust the online services (or the will kits from the Post Office), as per Professor Ries' advice. They can also act as your executor if you don't want someone in your family to have to do that job. More on that in Chapter 10.

- A **financial planner** can guide you if you're younger perhaps, and ones who charge a one-off fee (rather than a rolling commission on your portfolio) are best according to the experts. Banks usually have estate support lines to provide guidance, and in Australia we have the National Debt Helpline, which offers free financial counsellors to people in hardship.

- **Not-for-profits and charities** often have support lines, education events, and legal and financial services they work with to deliver information to their communities. If you have a particular diagnosis, there is probably a group dedicated to the care of people with that diagnosis (for example, the Cancer Council), or you might be (or become) a member of a community group such as a local Lions Club or Men's Shed, which might have connections that can help.

- **Social workers** are excellent referrers to services, and they can often help you put in place important directives. This might be through a hospital or service provider, for example. If they're available to you, use them.

Failing all of that, if you have a friend (or a friend who has a friend) who is a lawyer, accountant or just particularly astute, ask for their advice. You almost never have to do these things alone, and you can find an abundance of resources online to help. I know that abundance can be overwhelming, so I've put together a list of starters for you in the Resources section.

If you're still struggling to raise the topic with your loved ones, bring this chapter to the table and read it together. The point of getting your affairs in order is to pack the metaphorical box, put it under the bed and leave it there until someone needs it. You want it to be easy to find, easy to access and easy to navigate once you're inside. Then wrap it with a bow, because it truly is a gift to the people who will one day need to open it without you.

CHAPTER 10

Paper cuts

Dad is excitedly asking whether I know a song about New York that, unbeknownst to him, formed the soundtrack of my mid-to-late twenties.

'You mean the one with Alicia Keys? "Empire State Of Mind?"' I ask.

'Yes! That song came on as soon as I got in the car after I'd booked my flights,' Dad says, giddy with excitement and buoyed by a sign from either the universe or Jay-Z.

He has just booked a return trip to the US, a place that has been forever on his bucket list. As his daughter, I am delighted. As his carer, Enduring Power of Attorney and executor, I am concerned. My mind does a quick stocktake:

- **Concern 1.** The US has a notoriously expensive healthcare system, particularly for non-Americans.
- **Concern 2.** Dad has a pre-existing, terminal medical condition that precludes him from being able to get travel insurance.
- **Concern 3.** It's 2022 and COVID-19 is still running rampant globally, which is particularly frightening for someone with a compromised immune system and a degenerative lung disease.

Carer Casey parks her concerns to allow Daughter Casey to be happy for her dad. This is the trip of a lifetime, and I am not going to be the one to rain on that parade or any parade of Dad's choosing. Before he goes, I urge him to get his will in place. 'Just in case,' I gently plead, my worst-case-scenario brain doing its probably over-effective but nonetheless very important job of protecting us from being eaten by a metaphorical lion. In this case, the lion is the prospect of Dad dying alone, away from his family in a healthcare system that won't cover the costs for him. And the smaller, secondary lion—for me at least—is having to execute Dad's wishes with no will in place and his body overseas. It's not that there is much to divide but rather that trying to divide anything without legal documentation to do so is—I imagine—about as fun as peeling off your fingernails with a pair of tweezers. Current me is eager to avoid that for future me if at all possible.

Dad does as I ask and then emails me with the whereabouts of his will and some rudimentary instructions. I breathe a sigh of relief and then hold my breath for almost a month as Dad heads off on his adventure through the US. After stops in Melbourne, LA and New York, he arrives in Illinois, where he picks up a car and my older sister, then takes a road trip through Wisconsin, Minnesota, South Dakota, Wyoming, Colorado, Utah, Arizona and Nevada before eventually arriving in California. The trip is full of twists and turns—both literal and emotional—and to say I am relieved when he is back in one piece is an understatement.

Niagara Falls

While he is in the US, Dad attends a week-long intensive meditation retreat in Niagara Falls with a globally renowned neuroscience guru who touts the power of the mind to heal the body. I hold a complex position on events like this that's worth mentioning here. I am fully in support of learning to take advantage of the brain–body connection, and I won't make any argument against ancient tools like meditation being powerful for personal growth, stress management and mental wellbeing. What I am not in favour of is vulnerable people being misled by any sort of pseudoscience or the small number of cowboy, cowgirl or cow-person practitioners making unfounded claims within the incredibly lucrative 'wellness' industry. These people, probably with not-terrible intentions (most of the time), use people's fears around disease and death as a sales tactic. I'm not suggesting this was the case here, but I hear frequently about people forgoing proven medical treatments in favour of pursuing only alternative therapies because they've been influenced to do so, and it can cost them their lives. And in the world of largely unregulated social media, it's never been more important to keep that in focus.

I could write a whole book on this topic and barely scratch the surface, so I'm not going to dwell here. Instead, my hope is that reading this inspires you and the people you are caring for to:

- Make **truly informed decisions** on your own care for your unique situation.
- Know that **medicine isn't either/or;** there is room for both traditional and complementary or alternative therapies *if* you find them to be valuable.
- Ask your team to **act as a team,** so that our siloed healthcare sectors can better integrate with other, less-evidenced parts of the industry that support people's wellbeing in ways that may never be funded sufficiently to be studied and published in medical journals.

All that being said, I will also say this: if someone chooses not to make an informed decision, or to try to heal their disease with the powers of their mind, then that is 100 per cent their prerogative. It is their life and their choice. I'll also say that I absolutely saw the positive impact of the retreat's meditation training on Dad. He did walking meditations with 1500 people around Niagara Falls that I know moved him deeply.

Sadly, like most other intense learning opportunities, once any of us are out of that environment, the discipline required to continue the new-found skill tends to wane as the experience fades in the rear-view mirror. Still, Dad had some powerful meditations there and I can only hope those skills were valuable to him in the later stages of his illness and his life.

Potholes

In New York, Dad tours the actual Empire State Building, wanders the spiral staircase at the Guggenheim and admires the Statue of Liberty. He marvels at the Grand Canyon in Arizona, breathes in the mountains of Wyoming and peeks behind the curtain of LA life at the Hollywood Bowl, even taking in a Grace Jones concert. He sends us photos and videos and brings home souvenirs, silly things like mugs that would ordinarily become junk but, in the face of losing him, become treasures.

Like any road trip, the legal journey of wrapping up someone's affairs can be a straight road, with some necessary paperwork and a few stops along the way for gas (and snacks). But it can also be fraught, with potholes, dead ends and even a breakdown or two. It's easy to get lost because there isn't really a map, but having the right documents in place will make navigating those roads significantly easier.

In Australia, we are lucky to live in a country that has clear end-of-life documentation. Getting these documents in place while we are well—when we're making our best, clearest decisions—allows us to take some control over the inevitable.

Here's an overview of the documents we should all set up while we're still alive and able to do so.

Last will and testament

This is the bedrock of affairs and simply outlines who your stuff (and any children under the age of 18, as well as any pets) will go to when you die. It can be as simple as a one-pager, but it needs to be signed and witnessed by two witnesses who can't be beneficiaries of the will—so they can be total randoms but not someone who is due to receive anything from your estate. In this document you will choose and name a person to execute your will (the executor). This person will be in charge of ensuring your wishes are upheld, so you want them to be someone who is both capable and trustworthy. Ask their permission before listing them as your executor so they know you're expecting that of them. They must know where to find the *original* will document too, because while the aim is to never end up in court, a copy (even a certified one) is unlikely to stand up in court if they do.

If your situation changes, update your will and destroy any old versions. I can't tell you how many stories I've heard of people getting shafted by sneaky family members late in the game, or who have had everything go to the wrong person, rather than the people who loved and cared for the person who has died. The law isn't built on trust and goodwill, it's built on anticipating the worst-case scenario and protecting you from it. Remember the anvil in Chapter 9? Think about your situation—what's the worst-case scenario for everyone involved legally? The will's job is to prevent that and ensure the person who dies has the things they have worked hard to acquire over their lives go to the people—or causes—they choose. And if they choose for it all to go to the Cat Haven, that might suck for you but bravo to the cats.

Power of Attorney

Power of Attorney (POA), Enduring Power of Attorney (EPOA) and Enduring Medical Power of Attorney (EMPOA) are the three types of Power of Attorney documents you'll need to consider. Let's break these down.

- **Power of Attorney (POA)** is put in place to give someone the power to act on your behalf while you're still alive. They can make financial, legal and administrative decisions, but the power can be revoked at any time as long as the person they are acting on behalf of is of sound mind. For example, if you are travelling and unavailable, a POA can make decisions on your behalf like buying a house or selling your miniature pig farm business. If you were ever to lose legal capacity because you weren't of sound mind, the POA agreement would end.

- **Enduring Power of Attorney (EPOA)** gives someone the power to make financial, legal and administrative decisions on your behalf, *even if* you become incapacitated and aren't able to make such decisions for yourself. They can also make quality-of-life and medical decisions, such as placing you in a nursing home if that's what they feel is required. You can give them specific powers, such as operating your bank accounts, paying any bills or debts, and managing your financial affairs.

- **Enduring Medical Power of Attorney (EMPOA)** gives someone the power to make medical decisions on your behalf if you become mentally or physically incapable of deciding for yourself. It endures even if you have lost legal capacity, so again your EMPOA could choose to put you into a nursing home if that's what you need, or say yes or no to a specific treatment or intervention on your behalf. In some states, this person acting on your behalf is known as an **Enduring Guardian (EG).**

All three of these agreements (POA, EPOA and EMPOA/EG) end when the person dies (when an executor takes over), and it's worth noting that you can choose to have different people fulfil different roles. For example, you might give one person EPOA to handle your financial, legal and administrative decisions, and have another person act as EMPOA/EG to handle your medical and health decisions.

Advance health care plan/directive

This document sets out what medical interventions or treatments you want (including any quality-of-life parameters) for when you are unable to decide or speak for yourself. It covers what would be acceptable or unacceptable to you, and what medical treatments you would and wouldn't agree to. It may appoint a substitute decision-maker to make decisions for you (such as someone acting as EMPOA or EG), and it only comes into play if you can't advocate for yourself.

The point of an advance health care plan/directive is to make your wishes known to healthcare practitioners if you are unable to communicate, and alleviate the pressure on your family to make difficult decisions on your behalf. While you can't refuse basic comfort care (it can't say, 'Please leave me in a field to fend for myself like I'm on *Survivor*'), you can specify whether you would want common medical interventions, such as:

- Artificial feeding and hydration (a feeding tube, for example)
- Cardiopulmonary resuscitation (CPR)
- Assisted ventilation (a machine to help you breathe)
- Medications, like antibiotics
- Kidney dialysis (to filter your blood when your kidneys can't)
- Blood transfusions.

This document takes precedence over family wishes and only comes into effect after you lose capacity. You can revoke or change it at any time while you are still of sound mind.

Organ and/or body donation

Donating your body or organs to science or others who need them is a personal decision and will be dictated by your beliefs as well as your condition. Body donation needs to be arranged in advance, and whether the organisation you donate it to takes the body or not is up to the institution on the day you die. The family may or may not get any remains back to cremate or use in any sort of ceremony. Organ donation wishes have to be registered on the Australian Organ Donor Register, where you can choose which organs you'd like to donate (as in, heart—yes, eyes—no). Please note: Family can override your wishes at the time of death if they are too distressed or do not want to honour your decision. If it's important to you to donate your organs, then register as an organ donor—but also explicitly tell your family it's what you want.

In order for organs to be donated, the body needs to be kept oxygenated by a life support machine. If you die at home and your family want to spend time with your body there, you won't be able to donate your organs.

End-of-life plan

This could be called your end-of-life wishes or a death care plan. Basically, it sets out your hopes for end-of-life care and your body after death. It's the place to capture how you want to be communicated with, who you do (and don't) want involved in your care, where you'd like to be cared for, your cultural or spiritual beliefs, whether you'd like your family to have time to be with or wash your body afterwards, what you'd like in terms of body disposal (burial or cremation) and what you'd want in terms of ceremony. This is less a legally binding document and more a manifesto of your wishes to help your family deliver the sort of care and after-care you want.

An 'important things' file or document

This should contain your accounts, passwords and important contact details, as well as information on where all your important documentation lives—the titles for any property, your birth certificate, car registration, documentation of any shares you own or mortgages you hold—anything people might need. Someone trustworthy (ideally your executor) needs to know where that file or document lives and how someone could access it in the event they need to. You could give those instructions to someone in your family, a lawyer or trusted friend to hand over if and when the time comes. You could also include those instructions in your will, so they remain private until they're needed.

Choosing an executor

Given we're going worst-case scenario at this point (hard hat for hard chat), let's take this one step further. Once you have died, your will and executor step up and take over your affairs. If you had asked me prior to *being* one who you should choose, I would've said just pick someone you trust. However, now having been one, I don't know if I'd put that responsibility and workload on someone I love who is grieving me. I would probably choose someone I trust but who is slightly removed from my family, someone who would grieve me but not be deep in grief like my immediate family, someone who I know has the capacity and ability to execute on my wishes, and someone who I know would give up the many hours required to do so because they would see it as a gift to my grieving family. Again, that's a personal decision, but if you've never been an executor I'd think carefully about who you choose because it is a lot of work, especially when it involves selling property or vehicles and splitting assets. It's work that is usually done pretty soon after someone has died, when grief tends to be at its rawest. Trust me, I sat in the Department of Transport on the verge of tears for more hours than anyone should have to. You can also appoint more than one person to be executor, so the load is shared. And—to limit the chance of conflict—you can spell out exactly how you'd like them to work together.

• • •

Long before Dad died, we had a conversation about resuscitation. Until that moment he had been of the mindset that he'd have any intervention to stay alive a little longer. What he hadn't considered was the quality of life on the other side of that resuscitation. Our doula kindly helped him understand that cardiopulmonary resuscitation (CPR) isn't typically gentle. It can need to be quite forceful, and with a terminal, degenerative lung disease, that force would likely do irreparable damage to Dad's decaying lungs and ribcage. Even if it saved his life, that life would still be short and probably hooked up to machines in a hospital for the rest of it, pretty much dashing his chances of dying at home as he wished. After we talked it through, he changed his mind and put a DNR (Do Not Resuscitate) order in place. And there is research suggesting when patients watch videos of CPR, and see how intense it can be, they may choose differently too. Choice, and law, is all about knowledge and communication. Hard hat for hard chat.

CHAPTER 11

Dollars and sensitivity

For most of my life, Dad never had any money. We weren't sleeping on the streets, but he did take me to an abandoned, dilapidated mansion once where—if my memory serves me correctly—he suggested we live there as squatters. After a narrow escape from a giant hole in the floor, I politely declined. We weren't going hungry, but we were fairly reliant on local fast-food restaurants, two-minute noodles and other low-cost, low-nutrition food. For the record, I was as chuffed with this arrangement as my children would be today. I don't know if we were living below the poverty line—it didn't feel like that—but based on my calculations I suspect we were. I'm not trying to paint a poor-me picture here. My childhood was epic. I had two parents who loved me dearly, two warm beds, two roofs over my one head. I was loved, fed and cared for at both homes. Mum modelled a strong work ethic, hustle and financial stability, and Dad modelled backyard freedom, imagination and making money stretch. After rent, food and bills, there wasn't much left from Dad's welfare payment, and we would often hunt for coins under the couch cushions to put petrol in the car. I'm sure Dad stressed about money, but I didn't feel any of that—it was always more of an adventure. Dad was masterful like that.

It's not that Dad couldn't work—he could, and sometimes did. He was actually incredibly capable, still to this day one of the smartest people I've known. It's just that he could never seem to hold down a proper job for any length of time. He had skills and passions he'd dedicate to causes that were unable to pay him, instead finding purpose, passion and community in doing something good for the world rather than something that gave him a steady income with which to support himself and his family. It's a beautiful quality, and one that I'd guess drove his parents and the mothers of his children a bit mad, all of whom were left to do the majority of the financial providing. My armchair expert diagnosis suspects the reasons Dad couldn't remain gainfully employed are a complicated mix of unresolved childhood trauma, poor self-worth but strong self-medication, as well as a healthy sprinkle of depression, something Dad would later agree with but never choose to treat.

When he did apply himself, he was able to achieve some powerful things. We have a stretch of reef in Western Australia called Ningaloo — it's a World Heritage-listed site rivalling the Great Barrier Reef and home to one of the largest aggregations of migrating whale sharks, as well as manta rays, turtles and humpback whales. It's a well-kept secret and one of the few coastal treasures in the world that hasn't been overdeveloped within an inch of its life for tourists to come, enjoy and eventually ruin. To capitalise on its magic, developers had long wanted to build a marina at a site just outside of Coral Bay called Maud's Landing. Hearing about the development and already passionate about the health of our oceans, Dad ended up at the helm of what was called the Save Ningaloo campaign. With the help of notable and equally passionate Australians such as author Tim Winton, NBA (the US's National Basketball Association) champion Luc Longley, actress Toni Collette and local politicians, they were able to put a stop to the development, preserving the coral playground for generations to come. While this work didn't generate income for Dad (as far as I can recall), it did deliver impact for the community, and at a scale few of us can say we'll achieve in our lifetimes.

But when it came to any sort of wealth-building or even career-building, Dad never really did that. When he was diagnosed and I relocated to care for him, he was renting a tiny, cockroach-ridden apartment that wasn't government housing but was the cheapest he could find. Luckily his medical care was paid for by our public system, but outside of his pension and running the old car he bought with money from his super fund, there was very little left with which to live. You might recall me saying Dad's disease was due to exposure to asbestos, a diagnosis you'd typically see in people who work with the material, usually building or trade professionals or miners who dug it out of the ground back when that was legal. But Dad never set foot on a building site or even attempted any DIY, to my knowledge. Upon diagnosis, it was established that Dad had been exposed to asbestos at a specific age, time and location—and that there were a number of parties who were legally liable for that exposure. I'm treading carefully here (we are in the legal section after all), but the headline is that because of his exposure, and subsequent diagnosis, there was financial compensation available to Dad.

After a fairly straightforward but time-consuming process, Dad 'won' some compensation for his illness. It was by no means equal to the value of his life or even his suffering, but it was enough to allow Dad some comfort in his final days. He moved from the roach-riddled apartment to a cleaner, nicer, bigger one. He sold his old car and bought a brand-new one, something he'd always wanted to do. He bought a drone so he could take it camping and because why not, and he took us all out for dinner without thinking about whether he'd have enough money to pick up the bill. It was lovely to see Dad experience some financial comfort for the first time in my life, and while I'm sure he'd have given every dollar back to return the diagnosis, I also know he was grateful to feel like he'd have the chance to leave something for his children. Prior to that, Dad and I had a running joke that his five kids would split whatever we found behind the couch cushions—and we'd be lucky if we ended up with 50 cents and a pack of matches.

What the money afforded Dad was choice. The choice to buy a truck that could go off-road so he could go camping with his son. To go to therapy with his daughter. To bring my sister out from Chicago, and to take all five of his children up to Ningaloo—so we could stand at Maud's Landing and see the impact first-hand of what Dad's work was able to build (or, I suppose, *not* build). Just a vast, empty beach with a blue, blue ocean and an underwater aquarium we snorkelled, hand in hand, as a family. And I don't know if there's a price you could put on that.

When it comes to money and care, there's a lot we could cover here. Everyone's situation is different, but I think there are a couple of things we can agree on. The first is more tactical, being that money changes what sort of care you receive or can deliver, and that when someone is ill or injured that has a financial impact on both them and the person or people caring for them. It's measurable, like dollars. The second is that within families, money makes things complicated. It's sensitive. Talking about it can feel icky, and finances can be an absolute minefield within families, because in many ways it's the ultimate test of kinship. So, let's break these two areas down: dollars and sensitivity.

Dollars: The cost of care

There are many costs associated with care. There are hard costs, like the cost of delivering treatment—medications, medical equipment and devices, people power and the bricks-and-mortar buildings from which care is delivered. Then there are soft costs, like the value of the time carers spend caring for people they love, usually for little or no financial compensation, and the productivity lost when patient, carer or both are out of the workforce. These economics of illness and injury impact the public purse greatly, but they have a big impact on individuals too. And given you'll be navigating the mental load of money management while juggling everything else as a carer, you'll want to be aware of them.

Out-of-pocket costs

Even if medical care is covered by your public healthcare system, there are likely other out-of-pocket costs that come with giving or receiving care, things like:

- Transport (petrol, tolls, parking or public transport costs)
- Medications

- Additional supportive therapies or treatments
- Any gap fees your doctor might charge beyond what the government will pay for your appointment (if you're in the private system, there may be lots of gaps to pay, as well as the cost of the insurance to get private care in the first place)
- Nursing at home outside of what might be provided (for example, if your person is hell-bent on staying at home and requires 24-hour care that can't always be provided by family or friends, you'll have to find a way to cover that)
- Modifications to your car, home or even having to move house (like we did) to better accommodate the person's needs.

For most people these additional costs need to be managed carefully, as they add up, especially when coupled with loss of income.

Loss of income

You or the person you're caring for may not be able to work, and even if you're on a pension or disability benefit (or have income protection insurance), you might not be earning what you ordinarily earn. You may need to cut costs or change your lifestyle to accommodate the decrease in income. This might mean you need to roll out the dreaded 'B' word. I haven't yet come across a budgeting app specifically for carers, and the market moves too quickly for me to recommend any even if I had. What I do know is that crossing your fingers and hoping for the best isn't an effective strategy. Whether you use an app, spreadsheet, notebook or just your common sense and a calculator, you'll need to invest some time here. You'll have fixed expenses (like your mortgage, rent or childcare); variable expenses (bills that change month-to-month, like your power bill); medical/care-related expenses; and you'll also need some money to live your life. Only you can do the math on that for your unique circumstances and lifestyle, but do it in the knowledge that your two wealth levers—how much you spend and how much you earn—are likely to be affected during this time.

When it comes to financial support for carers, there is no doubt we need to revamp the way we fund and value the care economy—those who choose care as a profession and those who find themselves caring for someone they love. After all, care is the system that makes all other work possible. Ideally, care workers would be appropriately compensated for the vital work they do, and those who find themselves in the position of having to care for someone they love could choose between working and taking care of a young child, ageing parent, or ill or injured family member. Until care is better supported by public policy, depending on where you live and your financial situation there may still be some financial support available to you. In Australia, we have a number of carer payments to help support people providing care, including a carer payment and carer allowance, but even with these combined we're talking far less than minimum wage. It simply isn't enough, especially in a cost-of-living crisis. Where you live it may be an almost laughable stipend, but we need to work with what we can get. There may be not-for-profit organisations or charities you can apply to for financial assistance, as well as tax deductions for carers. Do your homework or ask a friend to help see what might be available to you.

In Australia, Carer Gateway is a great place to start. You can find the URL for their financial support page in the Resources section at the end of this book.

Moving backwards

With everything we do, there is a time–money trade-off. Choosing to become a primary carer (main carer) has a big impact on our earning potential and career momentum, which can directly impact our long-term financial position. This, especially as women, can affect our later-life security and safety. If you choose to care for someone you love it can mean less income, less (or no) super, loss of career projection and opportunities, plus a hole in your résumé. For some people, the choice to care is a no-brainer. For others, it's a much harder decision. For some, it isn't a decision at all—giving up work to care simply isn't an option. Those people have to bring in the income, face additional expenses *and* shoulder the burden of care. If that's you, you'll need to lean harder on the people around you and whatever support is available to you. (Also, please note that you are a hero).

If you do have the privilege of choice there is no right or wrong answer, and your decision will likely be affected by myriad financial, physical, emotional and career factors. If you have to (or choose to) keep working, consider asking for flexible work arrangements such as reduced hours, more flexibility or remote work. Know your rights and then use the tips we covered in Chapter 4 (on advocacy in terms of communication and relationship-building) to carefully negotiate so you can keep your job *and* take care of yourself.

Residential care

You may need to put the person you're caring for into a residential facility, like an aged care home. Depending on your financial position and which facility you want, you may need to pay a lump sum for this and/or a daily contribution that may or may not be means-tested (meaning if you have more income or assets, you may have to pay more up front). That can have a significant impact on your assets and cash flow. For example, the average buy-in fee (what's called a refundable accommodation deposit or RAD) is currently around half a million dollars but varies greatly depending on the location and facility. That's not small change.

Few of us keep these considerations in mind when we're planning for our financial future. We're often asked to think about how much super we need to retire, either by nosy friends or clever advertising. We imagine a future where the money we have slaved away for is dedicated solely to living our best lives: gifts for the grandchildren, pensioner movie tickets and maybe that cruise we've always wanted to take. But what if we—like most people in most developed countries—end up with a chronic disease that hinders us from living our best lives, and that pot of money is instead required to simply live? In Australia, around one in 10 bankruptcies are due to medical issues. In the US this figure is much higher, with more than half of personal bankruptcies associated with unforeseen healthcare spending.

But if you think about it, it's not really unforeseen. Most of our biggest killers—heart disease, dementia (including Alzheimer's disease), cancer, cerebrovascular disease (such as stroke)—usually come with a period of illness before they cause death, and these years, even if short, can be some of the most expensive of our lives. As we know that, we would be wise to account for it by setting aside some additional superannuation as an illness buffer. Because if we have to retire early due to illness, or we get ill or injured while retired, that may have a direct impact on our retirement savings, and therefore the quality of retirement we're able to have. And we're living longer in retirement than ever before, which makes decisions that can alter our financial position all the more important.

Sensitivity: Blood, water and money

The 19th century American humourist and philosopher Josh Billings once wrote that 'Health is like money, we never have a true idea of its value until we lose it.' To say I subscribe to this is an understatement. I've built a career on preaching that our health is our most important asset—that without it we have nothing. It's easy to say that when someone is ill, injured or dying, money doesn't matter—and in lots of ways, it doesn't. But in subtle ways, like the comfort it was able to deliver Dad in his final days, it does. And money is the currency with which we measure—rightly or wrongly—some much bigger themes: value, equity, justice, even love. So, in the context of losing someone you care about, money can become more important than it has ever felt before.

Some families follow a traditional pattern: one couple builds wealth and passes it on to their children, who build on that wealth and pass it down to their children, and so on forever. It's what keeps our rich rich and our poor poor. In these families, I imagine it can feel like a passing of the gold-plated baton: you have more to build wealth with in your lifetime, and some comfort—even if it's subconscious—that somewhere down the line, you have money coming your way. But most families don't follow this pattern, especially in a climate where fewer people are owning property, half of marriages are ending in divorce and we're reading books encouraging us to *Die with Zero*. Families are more modern and blended than ever, which raises very real challenges around blood, water and money. To say it can be contentious is an understatement.

Here's a little thought experiment.

Person A has a first marriage that bears one child, but that marriage collapses after 20 years. During that time, person A acquires a level of wealth that won't see them rolling around in a Maserati but will ensure they own a decent home and have some superannuation behind them for their golden years.

Person B also has a first marriage, from which three children are born. That marriage ends, but their circumstances are different to person A—they don't leave their marriage with any assets and live week to week.

Let's say person A and person B enter into a relationship later in life and fall madly in love, and two years later, person A becomes terminally ill. Excluding whether they are married or have a prenuptial agreement, should everything person A has acquired in their lifetime go to person B? Or to person A's only child? Or to person B with a view to then be split between their collective four children when person B eventually dies? What if person A and B had been together for five years? Ten years? Twenty years? What if they each had the same number of children? What if person A's child had nothing to do with their parent? What if one of person B's children provided all the care for person A? Does that alter your position?

Change any of these parameters—the relationships, the number of children, the length of time or timeline, the wealth built, the circumstances—and you'll get a glimpse into the reality of families across the world in any given moment. If you walked into any barbecue, I suspect someone there would have a story to tell about themselves or someone they know who had had things go wrong when it comes to family and money. Maybe they gave someone a loan they never got back. Maybe they found out someone was stealing from them. Maybe they learned the hard way that while money is a poor substitute for someone you love, losing it on top of losing them feels like a heartbreak double espresso.

On one hand, we know that money doesn't really matter at the end of life; you can't take it with you, so it doesn't hold any real value other than what remains for the people you leave it to. The complexity comes when we start to think of wealth as representative of that person's life and legacy. Of course, rationally we understand that children and impact are perhaps the most important legacies of all. But given care costs us — physically, emotionally and certainly financially — it's worth investing some time into thinking about how we future-proof not just our financial wellbeing, but our treasured relationships and anything that might negatively affect them. And money *can* negatively affect them.

This will vary depending on your care context, but if we're thinking worst-case scenario (which it would be smart to do), there are a few financial considerations for both you and the person you're caring for:

1. Having a rock-solid will in place that's witnessed and up to date, and that your executor knows the location of, as we explored in Chapter 10.

2. Having a clear idea of where your (or their) wealth is, with instructions for someone else to be able to execute on the estate should anything happen.

3. Being able to have honest conversations about money while we're still here to do so. As I've articulated previously in this book, this is not for everyone. Some people won't discuss money because it just isn't part of their belief system. But if you can have an open dialogue with your family, I think it makes the world of difference when you inevitably lose someone. If that person is terminally ill, this could include a conversation about any costs that might come up in their final years/months/weeks/days of life.

This third point is where Dad and I came up with an end-of-life budget, or perhaps because it's more catchy: a death budget.

This needs some context. When someone dies and their executor advises their financial institutions (bank, super fund and so on) that they have passed away, those organisations immediately freeze those accounts while they process the estate. This can take weeks or months. In the meantime, there are expenses to be paid. So, Dad and I put together a budget of all the expenses I would need to pay: his rent, bills and doula fees, plus the cost of his end-of-life celebration. We totalled up the projection and Dad transferred me that amount so I wouldn't be out of pocket while his estate was being processed. This is where an Enduring Power of Attorney can come in while someone is alive — paying bills and making sure the ill or injured person stays financially afloat, even while incapacitated.

If a death is unexpected and you don't have time to prepare, you can apply to your bank to release the funeral funds so you can at least pay for that while you wait for the estate to be processed. You may have to go through a process called probate depending on the size of the estate and what the rules say in your jurisdiction. Get an accountant or lawyer to advise if you aren't sure. There may be tax to pay on sales of assets, transfer fees for registration of vehicles and other expenses you might not be able to foresee. Again, seek financial advice and, if you can, have a buffer fund to cover these types of costs — or keep track, if you're the executor, so you can be reimbursed from the estate.

Dad had an idea that his nearest and dearest should all walk around his apartment and put stickers on anything we wanted. I think he thought it would be like *The Hunger Games* of belongings, a bit of fun in a not-so-fun time. Instead, we ended up just telling my siblings to say if there was anything in particular they wanted. Because Dad had never had much, there was no emotional connection to a family home we had to sell or precious heirlooms to squabble over. I posted a small bag of things to my sister in the US and everyone else just took a few items they felt connected to or might get use out of. We agreed the camping gear would remain in collective ownership and live in my garage for anyone to pick up at any time. No fights, no drama. We were lucky like that.

The rest of Dad's belongings got packed up and taken to his end-of-life celebration. We laid everything out on tables like we were at a 'Dad-market' and encouraged people to take home a piece of him. It gives me so much comfort knowing that the people who meant something to Dad have something of his sitting on a shelf, hanging in a wardrobe or hiding in a kitchen drawer. Tiny pieces of him everywhere that will eventually become parts of those families rather than knick-knack evidence of a life fully lived.

After Dad died, I commenced the great cancellation: cancelling all his subscriptions and billings one by one, and wiping his smartphone so I could gift it to his 90-year-old mother who was in desperate need of a new one. I struggled a little with that emotionally; it felt like I was erasing Dad's existence, at least technologically.

I'd get fun little executor surprises during this time too, like being charged for a health and wellbeing app Dad had purchased with my bank card for months after he'd died. The irony.

What would you pay for one more day?

We can crunch the numbers on how much it costs to place a stent in an artery, secure a room in an aged care facility, and even how much it costs to keep someone alive in their last year of life. But it is impossible to attribute a value to us. What is a life worth? Your life, my life, a child's life? What is a year worth? A week? A day? And what would we pay for more time?

Dr Anupam (Bapu) Jena is a medical doctor with a PhD in economics from Harvard. Over Zoom from Boston, he tells me that applying a financial mindset to illness and end-of-life decisions is common and necessary in medicine but impractical when it is attached to our incredibly powerful will to live, or when it could buy more time with the people we love.

'People look at that and say, "Wow, that's ineffective," because you just spent X per cent of your healthcare dollars on people who died—you should have reallocated that money and put it elsewhere,' he explains. 'And I think that logic is economically not sound.

You know, the majority of spending on refrigerators happens when refrigerators are about to crump. The majority of car spending happens when cars are about to fail. That's true for the human body as well, right? So it's not a surprise that a disproportionate amount of healthcare spending would happen at that point in someone's life.'

He tells me about a famous economist at the University of Chicago named Gary Becker who won a Nobel prize for applying economic analysis to human behaviour, and in particular a paper he published on the value of life near its end.

'The thought experiment that they gave was: if someone put a gun to your head and said to you, "How much would you be willing to spend for an additional day of life?" you'd say, "I'd give everything for a day of life." Put aside that you might have children or want to bequest it to other people, if you're dead the value of your money is zero to you. So you would be willing to spend an enormous amount just for very small extensions in life.'

Becker's paper and Jena's point is that while care costs — privately and publicly — a fortune, and even more so at the end of life, there's not much any of us wouldn't give for a tiny bit more time with our people. Doctors are no different, even though they know more about what may or may not work when it comes to end-of-life interventions: when they get there themselves, they behave just like the rest of us.

'It turns out they don't spend any less on [possibly futile] medical care than people who are not trained in medicine, which is surprising, right?' he tells me. 'The inclination of human beings is to push and to try because you never know what will happen unless you try, and doctors seem to exhibit those very same tendencies as everybody else. Human desire, a family's desire to spend as long as they can with a person and take a chance at that person being able to beat the odds; we always want to take that chance and that's a very difficult thing to fight against.'

So, we can take this very measurable metric — cost, spend, money — and measure it against the time it delivers, as well as what sort of quality of life we have. But what we can't value is what a life — or even a small amount of time — is worth to the person living it and the people who love them. Time for one more conversation, one more drive, one more question, one more hug. The value of those things is non-linear and therefore immeasurable, other than that most of us would pay anything we had for them.

This was certainly the case for Dad. In one of his many notebooks, I found a list of goals he'd written while on his trip to the US, and right at the top was:

MAKE A SPEECH AT CHARLIE's 18th

That's my littlest brother. Dad wanted more than anything to get him to 18, the theoretical threshold of boy to man. Just in case he didn't make it, we celebrated my brother's birthday early, and I'm so glad we did because Dad died at 8pm the night before Charlie turned 18, missing his birthday by a mere four hours. That's how I know Dad would've given anything for just one more day.

PART IV

Emotional Care

Making memories, death, dying and grief, celebrating life through ceremony and finding meaning.

CHAPTER 12

Homecoming

I am downstairs in the car park at Dad's apartment, emptying a bucket. *The* bucket that has been a constant at his bedside for months. Its job is to collect the tissues Dad spits the fluid into that his body rejects every morning after being horizontal all night. Because of the volume of scrunched tissues, the bucket fills quickly. I empty it every day, partially because I think it's more hygienic and also because I don't want it sitting next to Dad as a reminder of just how sick he is.

There's nothing noteworthy about this bucket. It's the kind of standard, run-of-the-mill bucket you'd pick up at Bunnings for a few dollars, bright red with a handle and lip—advantageous if you were using it to pour liquid. Today, the bucket is being uncooperative. On my first attempt, it almost empties but not quite. I turn it upside-down and tap the edge on the rim of the garbage bin, hoping the remaining tissues will dislodge themselves from the bottom of the bucket and find their rightful place. They don't, so I tap harder until the final tissue lets go, narrowly missing the goal of the bin and instead landing on me and then the floor. I sigh, bend down and grab it with my bare hands before putting it into the bin with more force than is probably necessary for a tissue. With poor spatial awareness on my best days and crippling, disorienting exhaustion on my worst, I turn to head back upstairs and catch the bucket between my body and the bin, which throws me off-balance and sends the bucket tumbling to the floor. It bounces, performs a perfect somersault and then rolls before parking itself in the middle of the driveway connecting the car park to the outside world.

I stare at the bucket for what feels like a long time but is probably just a few, intense seconds. In my body, all I can feel is anger. I am angry at any and all gods or whatever universal powers are at play in our lives right now. I am angry at cancer, at medicine for not being able to fix Dad and at his doctors for not understanding that to them he is a number, but to me, he is my dad. I am angry at asbestos, at his source of exposure, and I am angry at myself for not being able to work out a way to save him. But mostly, I am angry at the bucket. So, I do what any self-respecting adult would do—line the bucket up like I am David Beckham and kick it as hard as I can. It launches into the air, hits a wall with a crack and yet stubbornly refuses to crumple under duress, taunting me with its superior resilience and stupid handle. The irony that I am downstairs kicking the bucket while my dad is upstairs *kicking the bucket* is not lost on me. I say a silent prayer no one has witnessed or captured my soccer practice, then admit defeat by picking it up and reluctantly carrying it back upstairs, where I pretend that everything is fine, Dad isn't dying and I didn't just face off with a bucket.

Dad is sitting on the couch with one of his dearest friends. Both well over six feet tall, they are holding hands. It is heartwarming and beautiful to see two fully grown men—who aren't in a romantic relationship—in such an intimate position. They look at me as I walk in the door with glistening eyes and I realise they are watching *Homecoming*—the movie I made for Dad. While I only made it for him, I'm happy he likes it so much that he chooses to show it whenever he has a chance. As you've probably picked up through this book, Dad's life was a fairly colourful patchwork quilt. Lots of children, lots of lovers, much potential, much impact, but little tangible 'success' in the eyes of a society that still values the acquisition of promotions and possessions. Over some months, I interviewed the friends and family he loved most, scanned photos, carefully chose music and built out a 45-minute documentary for Dad. I hoped it would allow him to see his life through the lens of the big picture, rather than the ad-hoc chapters that make up our years but, in the moment, may not appear to fit together. I hoped it would make him feel proud of his life—what he had achieved, who he had loved and who had loved him.

I called it *Homecoming* because it's the name of the final step in a rite-of-passage weekend Dad often ran as part of his work with the ManKind Project, a personal development organisation for men that Dad was heavily involved with and strongly believed in. In many ways, this did feel like a homecoming—the ultimate homecoming. Perhaps if I could frame it as such, it would alleviate some of his distress. Sitting beside him on his bed while he watched it for the first time—both of us wearing his socks and eating ice cream with Maltesers—I saw him bask in the perfectly imperfect story of his life, which was one of the very best moments of mine.

'You're a giant human, you're a marvel,' he tearily said to me afterwards. 'You've helped me feel good about my life. I'm happy. I couldn't ask for a better testimonial.'

Touché Dad. As far as testimonials go, that one takes the cake for me too.

Watching someone you love change due to age, illness or injury is tough on the ticker. The Dad I grew up with was a superhero to me, with his movie-star looks, penchant for play and thirst for knowledge. I'm sure many of his children's mothers would do a silent, internal eye-roll to hear me say he tried his hardest, because their version of trying hard probably looked different to his. But I believe he did his best to build and live a life that resembled what a good life should look like. And yet for my entire adult life, I always got the sense Dad's head was just above water, and I could never quite put my finger on why that was. Poor self-worth and struggling mental health, perhaps, mixed with some disappointment that he'd never been able to make 'more' of himself. And we always, always want to make more of ourselves, no matter how much we have or do or are. There's always more to get and therefore there's always more to want.

Lights, camera, capture

I have always seen life through the lens of capture, long before we took photos of our breakfasts and sunsets and posted them for the world to consume. I find real life more interesting than fiction or drama, and in lots of ways believe we are all just playing out our own narrative. But that narrative rarely plays out the way we hope or dream it will. You can imagine my disappointment when none of my romantic relationships turned out like the movies, my real face and body didn't mature into the ones on the covers of magazines, and my first book didn't sell a million copies like it would've if I was the lead character on *Sex and the City*. And yet, the plot of my life (and no doubt Dad's as well as yours) has delivered more twists and turns than I ever could've scripted. That's how life keeps us on our toes.

Today, amid the arcs of my own life, I am always documenting. I jot notes in my phone, write, video, photograph and share some of that either online for the world to see or just in my family chat. I love having a record of what happened, who was there and how we felt about it. I probably got that from Dad, who was forever with camera in hand, and a prolific journaler and letter-writer. I can confirm this because I have a section in my garage dedicated to boxes of Dad's many, many journals—pages and pages of his thoughts and ideas and proof of his unabating desire to learn and grow.

So, it makes sense that I'd choose a career telling stories, asking questions and seeking answers. As a result, I've spent most of my professional life interviewing experts, usually in the health space—my favourite topic. When I started almost 20 years ago, the experts I interviewed still spoke fluent science, and my job was to take their convoluted, smart-person rhetoric and massage it into digestible messaging the rest of us could understand. Over the years, experts have gotten better and better at communicating with the public, thanks in large part to social media, and my job has become less about being a translator and more about being a trusted facilitator and intermediary. I am an expert at getting the best out of my subjects—making them feel comfortable enough to be open and vulnerable and share some of the person behind the expertise. It is an art, a good interview, and watching or listening to a great one unfold—I'm sure you can attest—is enthralling. There's highs and lows and you're on the edge of your seat for what comes next, all while feeling like you're in perfectly safe hands. It's thrilling to listen to, and even more thrilling to conduct.

One of the things people tell me after they've lost someone is that they wish they could hear their voice one more time, know what they'd do in any given situation and, of course, give them one more hug. After my mother-in-law died, we realised that while there were many photographs, there was very little video and even less of her voice captured for us to sink into when our hearts needed to. Like so many women, she was often the one behind the lens rather than in front of it. Still to this day, whenever one of us finds a clip with even a few words of her voice, we share it virally within our family chat for everyone to enjoy like the precious gold it is.

After that experience, I committed to interviewing my family—especially the ones I'm likely to lose soonest purely based on age. I've interviewed my grandparents (I'm still lucky enough to have two), my mum and my in-laws. My 85-year-old father-in-law answered a question a week from us for a year via email, added photographs for some colour and bound his answers into a book for us all—full of treasured family details that probably would've been forever lost with him if he hadn't captured them. And for my 40th birthday, just two months after losing Dad, I received a video from my best friend who had interviewed the people who loved me most, including—before he passed—my precious dad. It is a gift I will never, ever get over.

I firmly believe we should all interview the people we love most, because everyone has a story to tell. But we almost never take the time to ask the people we think we know best about their experiences and memories, and the lessons they've learned along the way. These interviews aren't just about gathering facts; they're an opportunity to truly understand someone's story in a way you probably haven't before. I've never done a family interview where I haven't learned something new, so think about this as a chance to capture some of what you don't know — a time capsule for future generations perhaps, as well as a keepsake for you. Don't worry about what to do with it afterwards, just get it down while you still have the chance.

You can use any medium you like, but I believe video captures their personality, beliefs and nuances far beyond what a photograph or the written word can convey. You get their voice, facial expressions, hand gestures, a sense of their values — the things that make them *them*.

You don't need to buy any fancy equipment, and this doesn't need to be a big song-and-dance production. You could capture them on the fly, at the park, in the moment. But if you do want to carve out some time to sit them down and interview them properly (which I couldn't recommend highly enough), here's what you'll need:

- **A smartphone.** You can use a video camera if you'd like to, I'm just about the lowest barrier to entry — and most of us now have a phone that can record video, many of which have high-grade, high-definition cameras that could stand up against most of the professional video cameras on the market.

- **Some decent light.** Natural light is ideal and it needs to be in front of the person you're interviewing so it shines on their face, not behind them as the camera will try to focus on where the light is, blowing out the shot and making your subject look dark. Failing that, you could point a few lamps in their direction, just try to avoid overhead lights on their own if you can. At the end of the day, you just want to be able to see them — don't overthink it, Spielberg.

- **A quiet space.** No wind, no screaming kids, no construction. Just a calm space where they feel comfortable and won't be distracted by noise. Phones should be on silent so you don't get interrupted, especially the one you're recording with (put it in flight mode or enable Do Not Disturb so any incoming calls don't stop the recording). If you have or want to use a microphone, you can, but for this purpose the microphone on your smartphone will be good enough.

- **A comfortable chair for them to sit in.** You want them to be seated in a way that allows their body to be relaxed and comfortable enough that they'll be able to concentrate on what they're saying, not distracted by why their lumbar spine feels pinchy. If they have a favourite chair, put them in it. If they're on a couch, make sure it doesn't look like they're being swallowed or sinking back into it. If they are, pop a cushion behind them to bring them forward. Some people like to be sitting at a table so they have somewhere to put their hands, just make sure they don't bang on the table too much when they get passionate. People do funny things when you turn a camera on them.

- **A comfortable chair for you to sit in.** You don't want to be standing beside the camera, hovering awkwardly or stretching because you got a cramp in your calf. Get comfortable in a chair that's set right beside the camera, with your eyes at the same height as both the camera and their eyes. (I talk more about your setup later in this chapter.)

- **Something to rest the phone or camera on.** This could be a tripod if you have one, but don't worry if not—you just want to be able to rest the phone on something. A table and a glass usually do the trick. Whatever you do, don't hold it. Even a tiny amount of movement can make watching it back unbearable.

- **Somewhere to store the files afterwards.** You can put them in the elusive cloud, on a hard drive or a computer, but have a backup somewhere that's not just your phone. Ask a tech-savvy person to help if you need to.

We'll talk more about how to set up the interview shortly, but before we get there, you're going to need some questions. What you ask will vary depending on who you're interviewing, but here are some ideas to help capture your subject's unique wisdom. Whether you're sitting down with a parent, grandparent, partner or dear friend, these prompts will help you uncover the stories that shaped them, like that time they bred budgerigars and sold them to pet shops for extra cash. It's not exhaustive but it's a good starting point, so take this list and curate it (or build it out) based on your knowledge of the person you're interviewing.

Remember, you'll need to use your common sense here. Avoid areas of questioning that you know are painful or sensitive.

First, ask them something generic to get them comfortable. Something like, 'Tell me a little bit about your early life; where were you born and to who?'

This allows them to talk about facts they know well but are rarely asked about. It'll help them get used to speaking to camera and may also give you some jumping-off points.

Here are some question ideas for the interview, with potential follow-up questions (+).

Early-life questions

- What were your parents like? Tell me about them ...
    + What was your relationship like with your father/mother?
    + Where did they come from (if they have a different country of origin)?
    + What was their upbringing like?
- (If they had siblings) What were your siblings like? Tell me about them ...
    + Who were you closest to and why?
- What is your earliest memory?
- What was your family home like?
    + What was your favourite spot in the house?
    + Did you have any pets?
- Did you have any family traditions or rituals?
- What was school like for you?
    + What was your favourite subject?
    + Do you remember any teachers who had an impact on you? Any awards you won? Any treasured friends?
- Were there any childhood experiences you think shaped you, for better or worse?

Career questions

- Did you always want to be an [occupation]?
  - \+ If so, when did you work that out? If not, what did you want to be?
- What were the best and worst things about your job?
- When you look at your industry now, what has changed from when you started out?
- If you had your time again and could be anything you wanted to be, what would you choose?
- Did you ever have a boss who really helped or inspired you? Tell me about them …
- Did you ever take a big risk in your career? How did it turn out?
- Is there a moment you can remember feeling truly proud of your work?
- Did you ever experience setbacks or failures? How did you handle them?

Relationship questions

- (If they have or had a long-term partner) Tell me about [partner's name]. How did you meet?
- What drew you to them/what did you like about them?
- What were the early days of your relationship like? Did you travel/work hard/have fun together?
- (If they've been or were together a long time) What have you witnessed in terms of their evolution in the time you've been together? How have you evolved as individuals and together?
- What do you think made your relationship work (or not work)?
- What challenges did you face as a couple, and how did you navigate them?
- What's something your partner does/did that always makes/made you smile or let you know they love you?

Parenting/family questions

- (If they have children) Tell me about your children. (Note: Spend some time here, as this is where most people will light up. Who are they, where were they born, who have they grown up to be?)
- What was it like becoming a parent for the first time?
- What surprised you most about raising children?
- What values do you hope you've passed down to your kids?
- What's a proud parenting moment that stands out to you?
- Does your family have any special traditions or rituals?
- How would you describe your family's sense of humour?
- What lessons has your family taught you?
- Tell me about one of the happiest times you can remember ... (this might be a family trip or a special memory).

Life questions

- When's the first time you remember feeling like an adult?
- Is there a motto, saying or set of words you live by?
- What do you draw on when you go through hard times? How do you overcome hardship in your life?
- What's the best piece of advice you've ever been given?
- What's something you've learned about yourself over the years?
- What's the one thing you wish you'd learned earlier in your life (or would still love to learn)?
- What's one thing you regret not doing yet?
- If you could speak to your 18-year-old self, what would you tell them?
- Have you ever had a moment where you completely changed your perspective on something?
- What's the most spontaneous thing you've ever done?
- Have you ever had a 'sliding doors' moment—where your life could have gone in a completely different direction?

- If you could relive one day of your life exactly as it happened, which day would you choose?
- What is the most purposeful or impactful thing you've done in your life?
- What do you want people to remember about you?
- What legacy do you hope you will leave behind?

Other juicy/random questions I like

- Tell me about a time when you felt really alive …
- Tell me about a time when you couldn't stop laughing …
- What makes you angry?
- What scares you?
- What's one of the most meaningful gifts you've ever given or received?
- What's the best compliment you've ever received?
- What's a smell, song or taste that instantly transports you back in time and where does it take you?
- If your life were a book or movie, what would the title be?
- Is there a particular place in the world that holds special meaning for you?
- If you had to sum up your life in three words, what would they be?
- What's your biggest wish for your family?
- If I gave you a magic wand and you could change one thing about the world, what would it be?
- Finish this sentence: When in doubt, _____
- What do you think makes a life well-lived?

The best last question is this: 'Is there anything else you want to say that we haven't covered?' It allows them to capture anything they want on film they may not have had the chance to speak to during the interview.

The setup

Before you get to the chat though, you need to set up your interview. There are a few considerations here.

- **Position of the camera.** You want to set up in front of your subject, with the camera facing them. Set up around two metres (six feet) away from them. When they are seated, the camera needs to be at their eyeline, so the same height as their eyes from the ground.
- **Position of you.** Sit a chair beside the camera, quite close to it (as close as you can get). The camera and your eyes need to be at around the same height.
- **Framing.** As long as they're in frame, it'll work. But if you want to up-level the look and feel, you want them to be in between what the film and television industry would call a medium shot and a medium close-up (or MCU if you're feeling fancy).

I like to go between because it captures more of their gestures, particularly their hands. Make sure the camera is landscape, not portrait—meaning horizontal (like a TV) rather than vertical (like TikTok or Reels on Instagram). Unless you are specifically capturing video to share on those social media platforms, you're better off recording in a way that will play best on a computer screen or TV.

You have two options to get the framing right:

1. Place the camera at the distance that gives you the desired framing.

2. Use the zoom function (in or out). I prefer not to use the zoom because on some phones you lose quality, but do whatever you need to do. If your phone has the functionality, you can try putting it on 'cinematic' mode or similar—this will blur the background slightly and make it look more professional.

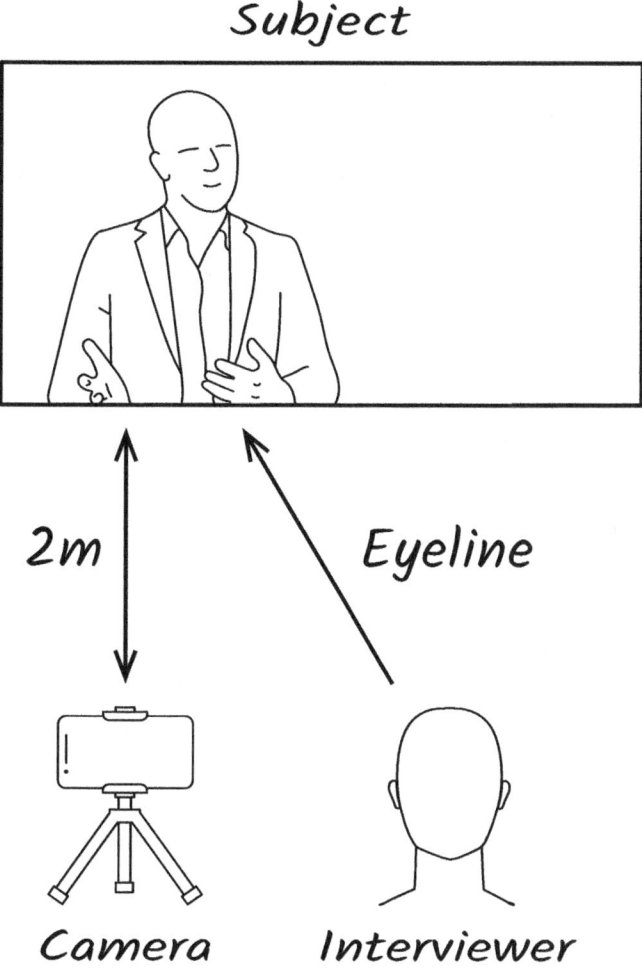

Subject

2m

Eyeline

Camera

Interviewer

- **Eyeline.** This is important—they should be looking at you, not at the camera. For the vast majority of us, looking at a camera is akin to public speaking—a fear greater than death. You'll get a much more natural result if they're looking at and speaking to you. Tell them to ignore the camera completely. This will give you a nice 'off camera' feel that is best practice for these types of sit-down interviews. Their whole body should be angled slightly towards you, not just their head and eyes. Get them to point their knees and chest towards you too; they'll get uncomfortable quickly if they feel like a pretzel.

- **Wardrobe.** Tell them to wear something they feel good in. Trust me, after they're gone you won't care if they were in their best clothes or their sweatpants, with makeup on or messy hair. Small patterns in clothing tend to 'strobe' on camera (it confuses the lens and can look blurry) so block colours are best, or big patterns are usually fine. You want it to be reflective of them, so if they are known for wearing their Victoria Bitter singlet then they can wear that. They want to feel like themselves, and for memories' sake you want them to look like themselves too.

- **Give them a glass of water.** For obvious reasons! Our mouths get dry when we're nervous, so make sure they have something nearby to wet the whistle.

- **Then, hit record and capture the whole thing.** Don't stop recording between questions unless they need a break. This will make your life easier in the future when you're hunting for the file as it'll be a long video in the mix of short clips that tend to make up our galleries. It does, however, make transfer to a secondary location harder because of the file size, so if you want to break it up you can—I just find it interrupts the flow of conversation.

You might need to do some coaching, given they aren't used to being interviewed. First, reassure them this is just for fun—there's no pressure. There's a good chance they'll be feeling nervous, self-conscious and a bit shy, so anything you can say to calm them down a little will probably get you a better result. If they don't know an answer, they can skip it and move on. If they want to stop or redo something at any time they can. My best interviewing tip took me years to work out and it's this: get a loose idea of your questions, then put them to the side and focus on listening. This is just a conversation, and you've been conversing for most of your life. Really listen to their responses; see where you might dig a little deeper or back off where you need to. Watch their demeanour and bring your knowledge of them into play. Tread carefully where you know you should; this isn't an interrogation piece on CNN. Your questions are there for you to draw on when you need them, but try to be in the moment and let the conversation flow naturally for a better result.

Here's an example. Let's say your interviewee starts talking about someone called Peter. Your next question was about their work, but later in the piece you had planned to ask them a question about Peter. They've just opened the door, so walk through it: 'I was going to ask you about Peter...tell me a bit more about him.' You can come back to the work question afterwards. In short, don't be too rigid. Just chat. I prefer not to give people the questions ahead of time—it tends to make them overthink their responses and they can come out sounding too rehearsed. Off-the-cuff reactions are usually more natural and deliver better responses. But again, you know your person best—and if they want to see them beforehand, let them. They might feel more confident if they can prepare. Reassure them that this is just a conversation, so they can forget about the camera and the questions and just chat to you. The more relaxed they are, the better they'll be (and the more they'll enjoy it).

I have hours of footage of interviews with Dad, audio recordings of our conversations and snippets of him reading to my children or cheering on my siblings at sporting games. I rarely revisit them in great detail, but when I do I feel like I've just had a conversation with him. These captured moments are the closest thing I have to being able to spend time with him, and they are more precious to me than anything I own.

The last question in one of our big, sit-down interviews is: 'What do we do when we miss you?'

Dad's response is textbook him: a joke, followed by some of the wisest words I could've asked for.

'Drink and smoke?' he offers with a giggle.

'I don't want that for you. I don't know, get over it? Loss and grief and sadness and the things that we love and think are vital to us all have a use-by date. All fall away eventually, and in those moments, all we can do is reach into ourselves, resource ourselves, and go "I got everything I could from that. There is no more to be had, no more that can be given. That end point had to come so I could start here."'

I tell him I love him, he blows me a teary kiss and I come in for a hug. All captured on camera.

CHAPTER 13

Low tide

A quick note before we get started on this chapter. While I highly recommend familiarising yourself with this information well before you need it, this is the point where I talk about dying, death and what comes next. If you're not there yet, you're welcome to come back to this chapter when you need it. Otherwise, it's worth sticking around.

There is no word for the last month of Dad's life other than brutal. In an extended state of what's known as terminal restlessness, Dad cannot be still. It's as though if he sits, sleeps or stops, death will catch him. So, we move. Day and night we walk anywhere and everywhere. When Dad's feet are so swollen with fluid shoes no longer fit, we go barefoot. When the café gets too far, we push him in the wheelchair. When getting out gets too much, we shuffle the hallway: up and back, up and back, up and back. To those watching, his body seems desperate to surrender to rest, but death is a fate his mind simply won't allow.

One night, after dark, we are on our third lap of the hospice grounds—Dad barefoot and arms interlinked with mine.

'Be honest with me. Do you really think I'm getting out of here?' he asks me tentatively.

I inhale into the space between his question and my response. I take a micro-second to consider my choices—be honest or tell a kind lie. Given we have spent a week in hospice and so far no one has said any of the 'D' words — death, dying, die, dead — I choose honesty.

'I do, Dad, but I think that realistically you're probably not going home for a bunch of good weeks...' I say, also carefully avoiding the D words but trying to give him the truth he is clearly craving.

'Well, that's giving it to me straight,' he bristles. 'I thought I'd give it a good fist...'

He trails off, I try to overcompensate with platitudes and then our conversation turns quieter — him going inward to reflect on what I'd said, and me going inward to reflect on what I'd said. I regret my response almost immediately, and will come to spend countless hours picking apart every word and ruminating on what I could have done differently. Here's a snapshot of my internal self-talk.

Why didn't I just end my sentence after 'I do, Dad'? That was the truth, I *did* think he was getting out of there. *Why oh why* did my mouth keep going?

***Realistically?* What, like he's not being realistic? He's dying, for god's sake. That's as real as it gets, you idiot.**

A *bunch* of good weeks? Are we talking about grapes? What the actual f*ck Casey.

While my inner monologue was vicious, I hold a lot of compassion for that version of myself. She'd been white-knuckling through 'the last weeks' for a year. It felt like none of Dad's healthcare professionals were being brutally honest with him about where he was at, and he was looking to me for the truth. I am not a therapist or psychologist or even very good at paying my bills on time, and I was way out of my depth — swimming alongside someone who was drowning, panicking and holding on to me literally and figuratively as though I was an island in a stormy sea.

Dad's relationship with his demise was unsurprisingly non-linear. He didn't follow the stages outlined by Swiss-American psychiatrist

Dr Elisabeth Kübler-Ross's seminal work *On Death and Dying* — denial, anger, bargaining, depression and acceptance. While this work was historically significant, marking a cultural shift in conversations about death and dying, it was long misunderstood as people reporting on it tried to fit the overly messy experience of dying into a neat, logical framework. Still, I love a framework. And I was probably secretly hoping Dad would follow one, so I could follow it too. Instead, he did what I suspect all dying people do and dipped in and out of each of those stages plus a number more — sometimes within the hour.

Sometimes, he was philosophical, practical and outwardly full of acceptance.

'It's an interesting dilemma, paradox almost,' he told me. 'To be accepting of death and what's clearly coming and what the medics are saying and the information I'm reading, and at the same time fighting if you like or doing everything I can do to give my body every chance of lasting another week or month or whatever.'

Others, he was outwardly full of fear — pushing me away when he needed to but wanting me close almost always, as though if we just held hands hard enough I'd be able to hold him in this world, even though the next beckoned stronger than any amount of muscle could withstand.

Finish lines

In the final days, I watch Dad's prized mind fall apart. He wants to go to the butcher for mince. I say we will. He asks if my brother is coming with 'the gear'. I say he is. He tries to eat my iPhone with a knife and fork. I silently replace it with a bowl of soup and, most importantly, a soup spoon. He is quiet, frightened and occasionally angry. The closest person to him, I bear the brunt of that anger, and while I try not to take it personally, it's becoming impossible to separate the person from the disease and it hurts. He feels ripped off, and I get it because I feel ripped off too.

Nurses come to the house every few hours to give Dad more and more medication — terminal sedation to allow his body to go through the process of death without causing his spirit too much distress. The medications get stronger, the doses get higher and, eventually, they insert one pump followed by another to deliver medication subcutaneously (through the skin), then a catheter to reduce the risk of falling on a trip to the bathroom.

Getting him into a restful state drains every last ounce of my wellbeing and makes my humanity wobble like jelly, as I balance the clear and medically informed need to get him comfortable with him not being ready to rest. The nurses are gobsmacked; they tell me they have never seen anyone with this much medication in their system still trying to get out of bed. It is too dangerous to let him get up in case he falls or falls on one of us, so we have to gently hold him in the bed to get him to calm down. If my heart was broken before, it is annihilated now.

That night, I gather everyone to the house. Dad is sleeping now but complaining about it by breathing loudly—the 'death rattle' warning that the end is imminent. I'm certain he can hear us around the dinner table and is desperate to join us one last time. We're all there—his mum, kids, grandkids and his death doula. After dinner, I go in to see him and I can see his breath changing, like a tide slowly washing out. I ask the doula if it's happening, and she says it is. I take his hand in my hand, my other hand on his chest. I say things like, 'It's okay to go Dad, there is no more to be done, we love you.' He takes four big breaths, moving his head over his shoulder like he's doing freestyle between the world he's in and the one he's heading to. Then he takes two smaller breaths and, with a quiet exhale, he is gone.

The room feels both achingly empty and bursting at the seams with the gravity of what has just occurred. A moment 68 years in the making.

I remember in the lead-up to Dad's passing it was really important to me that I was holding his hand at the end. I don't know why; I'd like to think I would've given it up for my siblings if they needed it, but for some reason, I knew that of his two hands, I needed one of them to be mine as he left the world. Maybe it's that I knew it would be the last time I'd hold my fiercest protector's hands. The same hands that cut my umbilical cord, handmade me a medal the first time I swam 50 metres on my own, and held my hand everywhere we went, even as I grew into an adult.

At the doula's suggestion, we open the windows so his soul can leave the room, then each put on one of his favourite tee shirts and wash his body, talking to him as his skin changes colour and turns cool. I ask my siblings if they want me to call the funeral directors to have his body removed that night, and my littlest brother, four hours from turning 18, asks if we can keep his body until tomorrow so he can see his dad on his 18th birthday. My children kiss Dad goodbye, and my husband takes them home so Dad and I can have one last sleepover. I wake frequently in the night, candlelight still dancing on the roof and walls around the shadow of Dad's hospital bed. He is *right there*. And all I can think is all the words the healthcare professionals never used. They all come out to play at once, finally freed from playing hide-and-seek: *My dad died. My dad DIED. My DAD died. MY dad died. MY DAD DIED.*

Death is, in many ways, many people's greatest fear. There's an unimaginable—to our imaginative minds—finality to it, laced with the inescapable reality of not knowing what comes next. While some claim to have 'seen the light', no one has gone and come back again, as far as we know. We don't know what comes next; we just have our beliefs to go on. We can agree that the body dies, but what happens after that is unlikely to ever be known. I have certainly never died, so I suppose this entire chapter is a fool's advice. What I can tell you is that watching someone you love die is heartbreaking, but seeing them leave their struggling body and suffering behind is painfully relieving.

In Ghanaian-American death doula Alua Arthur's beautiful book *Briefly Perfectly Human*, she explains that societally, we shun conversations about death, pretending we have control over disease and therefore over our lives.

'Human beings are funny that way,' she writes. 'Our clear inadequacy and powerlessness in the face of death is a reminder of our limitations. And understandably, that is scary. But the idea of death is a seed. When that seed is carefully tended, life grows like wildflowers in its place.'

It reminds me of something Zenith Virago, the deathwalker I introduced you to in Chapter 6, once told me.

'When someone is ill, you always set a place at the table for death,' she explained to me. 'You just don't feed it.'

I love this analogy, because it allows for the possibility of death—and death is always a possibility, whether we're chronically ill or a beacon of wellbeing, and whether we're nine or 90. When I interviewed Zenith in a Brunswick café, we sipped coffee and waxed lyrical about life, death and everything between, and she said something I've carried with me ever since.

'When people are dying, one of two things tends to happen,' she shared. 'Some people expand into love, and others contract into fear.'

I admit that when people use language like 'expand into love' my brain tends to enter some sort of protective short-term coma. I have limited capacity for 'woo' and have historically preferred to use my limited attention span for science over spirit. But, having gone through the experience with Dad, I can't tell you how true this turned out to be. When Dad was angry, rude or distant, I could smell the fear on him. When he was going out of his way to be kind, generous or affectionate, he was pure love. Knowing he could be either on any given day/hour/minute felt like a superpower, like I had X-ray vision that made his understandably unpredictable behaviour easier to navigate and harder to take personally. It wasn't just Dad; I felt the love and fear in me too. Perhaps—especially when we're faced with the monstrous challenge that is being a carer—while we're very good at expanding into love, we could get better at noticing when we're contracting (and reacting) out of fear. I know I could've.

My fear manifested as control. I thought that if I organised, orchestrated and optimised every element of our lives with schedules, plans and backup plans, perhaps I could grind our way out of this. If I just dedicated myself fully and worked as hard as I could, maybe, just maybe, I could save him. Which of course, I could not. But fear often isn't rational, and I'm not ashamed to admit that I have been deeply afraid of death. Not the actual dying part—I have faith that can be managed well by our medical system to prevent distress. But more that there will come a day I won't be here anymore. I don't want to not be here. I like being here. It's taken me a long time to like myself, and like my life. I'm terrified that now I do, my time will be cut short to punish me for so many years of taking my brain/body/ privilege/opportunity for granted. See? Irrational.

That time a doula saved my life

It's not surprising that personally and professionally I've been drawn to thinking and talking about dark themes such as death and palliative care. It fits my model of 'knowledge is power'. And while I can't say my fear of not being here is cured, I can say having a front-row seat to the profound experience of someone's death—and the knowledge I acquired on the way—has made me more comfortable with the process we will all inevitably go through. What made the biggest difference, though, was having someone walk beside me who had been there before.

I told you we engaged a death doula to deliver spiritual and administrative guidance to Dad not long after he was diagnosed. You might've heard of doulas in the context of birth—a cheerleader and support person who helps and advocates for parents (particularly mothers) through pregnancy, birth and the postnatal period. As I learned, death is not unlike birth—there's a logic the body follows. Just like during birth, in death the body is flooded with hormones to assist it (as it is during orgasm, or *la petite mort*—the little death, as the French so perfectly put it). Our doula helped us understand death better, prepare for it as best we could and know what to do after it, which can be an absolute nightmare when you don't know what you're doing, as I most certainly did not. There is an enormous amount of admin that goes into transitioning someone out of the world of the living and into whatever comes next. Understanding these processes and being able to communicate their nuances to someone navigating them for the first time is where an end-of-life doula shines, and ours brought more value to my experience than I could ever put into words.

Due to my woo intolerance, I wasn't sure I'd gel with our doula — all dreadlocks, patchouli and quiet knowingness. But with 25 years' palliative care experience under her belt as a nurse, she expertly fielded my million clinical questions and opened my eyes, mind and heart to the spiritual side of care. We engaged her to guide Dad through losing his life, but when he couldn't go there emotionally (hello, fear) she turned her attention to saving mine. When I needed time off from Dad's care to mother or work, she was my respite. When I was lost, she was my compass — orienting me in the maze of our health, death and aged care systems. And when I fell apart, she gently put me back together and assured me I could keep going.

Advocating for someone who is dying gets harder as disease takes over: they may become less sure of what they want and less able to communicate those wants. As a result, sometimes you can feel like you are advocating against them — balancing wish with need. Translated: sometimes your suggestions and decisions can piss them off. Having someone to debrief, decompress and dismantle the hard days with isn't just helpful — it's imperative. While they can't use their hands-on clinical skills in their capacity as a doula, if you can find one with a background like nursing it makes them an invaluable sounding board and resource to translate medical advice if you don't speak fluent medicine.

Birth and death are the biggest transitions we will ever go through, and while there are people available to help us organise and navigate almost every other aspect of our lives, there is no one to help with the biggest transition of all — to explain what to do and which order to do it in. Dad was not the first person to die, and he certainly wouldn't be the last. So why did I feel completely alone in navigating this? Enter: a doula. Having someone to guide you who knows the landscape is like hiring a captain to drive a boat — smart and kind of essential to your survival. If you are on (or caring for someone on) an end-of-life journey, I can't recommend hiring a doula enough.

Here's some of what ours was able to help me navigate, captured as a list to help guide you through some of the unchartered territory you may encounter—whether you choose to engage a doula or not.

Before death

There is a window of time prior to death that is unique, because—if they are well enough—you have access to buy-in from the person who is dying. Once the window is closed, it is closed. So, if they're open to it, here's what I'd try to talk to them about now.

❏ Understand where they—ideally—would like to die: home (which may or may not be possible depending on their condition and the level of care you and your family can manage to provide), hospital or hospice. Bear in mind here that while we use the term 'hospice' for a place people go to for end-of-life care, hospice is actually a theory of care that focuses on comfort and quality of life for people who are terminally ill. Hospices themselves are incredible places, and while hospitals tend to see death as failure—they exist to keep people alive so are more likely to intervene at the end of life—hospices and palliative care services see a good death as a success. Because sometimes the concept of 'healing' can be leaving a sick body behind and transitioning to the next place. Home can be beautiful, but it can also be incredibly hard on the people saying goodbye.

❏ If they'll discuss it, find out what sort of death they want. Do they want to be alone or have people with them when they are dying? If so, who do they want (or not want) there? Do they want music playing? A marching band? Some of this might be captured in their advance health care plan/directive (refer to Chapter 10), but find out what they want while they're well enough to tell you.

❏ We got our funeral director in place prior to Dad passing—in fact, he met with them. The first one we met with told us it would be inconvenient for them if Dad died at home, because his body wouldn't fit in the lift on a gurney, and the stairs would be difficult for her staff to navigate. I tried to practise compassion for her clear swing-and-a-miss, as I imagined in her line of work she'd become desensitised to death, but I'd be lying if I said I didn't also silently wish a small pony would kick her in the kneecaps. While meeting funeral directors is not for everyone and every circumstance, having them in place can help inform the process and gives you one less decision to make in the direct aftermath of a death, which I was glad for when the time came. The morning after Dad died, I contacted them and they helped chaperone me through what needed to happen next.

❑ Start making a list of people you know they would want at their funeral or ceremony in advance, with their contact details. If they're open to it, you can ask them directly and build the list together. Otherwise, just start taking note of the people they are communicating with or wanting around—this gives you a good idea, and it's better to do before they are gone rather than trying to remember once they are. I still feel guilty about friends of Dad's I missed reaching out to because I wasn't thinking clearly. They deserved an update, and my foggy brain wasn't able to give them one.

❑ On that, perhaps set up a 'need-to-know' text group with everyone on it your person wants updated as things unfold. Then you have one channel through which to update the group as you need to, so it doesn't become an onerous task for you.

❑ Make sure you know where all their important information is held—this will save you a mountain of headaches. Chapter 10 runs through all the key documents you need to have at hand.

❑ Know that some people experience what's known as the 'death rally', where—after a period of decline or lack of lucidity—they can seemingly rally (as the name suggests) and appear to be turning a corner. This can be a nice time for family to reconnect with their person, but it can also be disappointing when they aren't prepared for the inevitable, subsequent re-deterioration. If you get it, embrace it. It's a little gift before they go.

During death

From what I understand, death is as unique as the person doing the dying. But in the final stages of life (what's called 'actively dying', or when they are dying imminently), a few things may occur.

- **Appetite and thirst decrease.** They may have little desire to eat or drink, which is more concerning to the family than it is the dying person. It is part of the process—the body is shutting down, and they will naturally want to stop fuelling it. Sips of water or chips of ice, a moist mouth swab or some lip balm can help with mouth dryness and keep them comfortable.

- **Alertness is swapped for sleep or drowsiness.** They may spend more time asleep or very sleepy, and may not want to be woken. Let them rest as their body prepares to undergo its most important transformation yet.

- **Temperature can change.** The hands and feet especially can become cooler, with less blood flow; for others, they might be hot and clammy. They could look blotchy or dark in colour. Use light bedding; don't overcook them. If they are hot, gently apply cool, damp cloths. Be subtle—too much of a counterbalance in temperature can make them uncomfortable. Make sure the room is well ventilated but not drafty.

- **Incontinence.** As people drink less, their urine may become darker in colour. The less they eat and drink, the less their body needs to expel, and when getting up to use the toilet is no longer possible, pads may be required (or the medical team may insert a catheter).

- **Secretions.** As the swallow reflex slows down, saliva and mucus can gather in the throat, causing a gurgling or bubbling sound sometimes known as the 'death rattle'. This can sound stressful to us but it doesn't usually distress them. You can raise their head on pillows or turn them on their side to help. Medication can also be provided to slow down saliva or mucus production.

- **Breathing.** Their regular breathing will change. Breaths may be fast, slow with big gaps or inconsistent. They may be shallow or noisy. It'll look and sound different to their regular breathing.

- **Hearing.** Hearing is thought to be the last sense to go, so if you think it's appropriate you can play some calming music or speak to them gently. You can hold their hand, stroke them softly—whatever feels right.

- **Struggle.** They can hallucinate, try to get up and run away—anything is possible. Medications can help calm the body to allow it to go through the process. From what I understand, this is far more distressing to the people around them than to the dying person.

- **Death.** Once they die, their breathing will stop completely. They will have no pulse or heartbeat. Their mouth and eyelids may be open, and their pupils will be fixed. You can gently shut these, if you'd like to. Once they die, don't rush into doing anything. Be present. There is nowhere to be, nothing to do in this moment. Just be with them.

A note here. Whenever I asked the hospice doctors how long Dad had left so I could prepare myself and our family, the answers would vary wildly between who I asked and when I asked them. One doctor would say three months, the next would say days to weeks. I found myself wondering why no one could tell me if he had a month, a week or a day to live. Wasn't this their area of expertise? If dying is a process every single person on the planet will go through, why were we so in the dark? In lieu of any consistency of the guidance from our medical team, I found myself googling signs of death frequently, much of which has been provided here so you don't have to hunt for it like I did. And now? I wish I'd put down my phone and just been there, for whatever time it was.

After death

After someone dies an expected death, there are several steps that need to take place. If they die in a hospital or hospice, you will likely be ushered through these steps by the team there. But if they die at home, as Dad did, knowing these steps is helpful. I'm mindful that putting the following into steps is like trying to put together a seven-step framework for religion. But there is a lot of time after someone dies when you may be thinking, 'What do I do now?', so this has been provided for that purpose—to point you in the right direction.

Step 1: Someone needs to verify the death. This is usually an attending doctor—either the dying person's GP (general practitioner) if they have one or someone from the palliative care team. When you are ready, call whichever doctor you have been working with (they can direct you if they're not the right person). A doctor will visit to confirm the person's death and issue what's called a medical certificate of cause of death (MCCD), which usually needs to be done within two days of death. This is your ticket to proceed, so to speak. If there is no doctor available, an authorised nurse or paramedic can complete a verification of death form. Please note there is no rush here; if they die during the night, you can wait until the morning before calling a doctor. You don't need to contact the ambulance or police services for an expected death that occurs at home. If you don't know who else to call and you have already appointed a funeral director, they should have given you an all-hours number to call and can help here.

Step 2: When (and only when) you are ready, someone will come to collect the body. Some cultures keep the body at home with them until burial, others prefer to have the body taken away quickly. You can be with the body at home for as long as you'd like. You can cuddle them, touch them, talk to them. Some people like to wash the body (like we did) and change their clothes so they go off in their favourite outfit. If you move the body (rolling them to dress them, for example), their lungs can expel air—it sounds like a sigh and can be disconcerting if you're not ready for it. Keep the room cool and remove any blankets to keep the body temperature low, especially if the weather is warm.

If you are working with a funeral director, they will likely come and retrieve the body. If you don't have one yet but are planning to use one, that could be a good thing to organise now. They will store the body for you until the time comes to dispose of it by burial or cremation. You don't have to work with a funeral director, and your doctor or local palliative care service should be able to advise you on next steps if that's your choice.

Step 3: From here, you can report and register the death with the relevant body, which in Australia is the Births, Deaths and Marriages registry in your state or territory. When you register the death, you will receive a death certificate. If you are working with a funeral director, they may do this for you. If you aren't, the person taking charge of the funeral will need to register the death.

I found I worked on steps 4 and 5 simultaneously.

Step 4: Now it's time to plan their ceremony if they are having one. You might already have some ideas in place as communicated via their end-of-life plan (refer to Chapter 10). The big-ticket items here include finding a venue and celebrant, setting a date and letting people know. You might have a small, intimate, invitation-only ceremony; a large, public ceremony, where anyone who feels called to can attend; or no ceremony at all. You might have a private cremation and no ceremony, or you might have an unattended cremation and then a celebration-of-life party. Hopefully, you'll have some direction on their wishes to follow so you have fewer decisions to make. More on this in Chapter 15.

Step 5: You'll need to commence the long, winding road of wrapping up their affairs—especially if you are the executor. I would sit down—perhaps get a friend or family member to help—and do a brain dump of everything you can think of that needs to be done. You'll forget things, but if you get a list started you can add to it as you think of things. Break big tasks down into smaller tasks. Before you know it, you'll have quite the list. I've made a start here for you to help.

These are in no particular order, but broken down into financial, medical, digital/technological, practical and social tasks. I've written them assuming you're the executor; if you're not, some may not be applicable.

Please note, everything on these lists took me the better part of a year to complete. There are some things I still haven't done, and I include them here so you don't miss them like I did. But please don't put too much pressure on yourself. Tick something off whenever you're able, and delegate if you can.

Financial

☐ **Locate important information:** Track down their birth certificate, will (for their executor, which may be you), titles to any ownership of property or vehicles, insurance policies, superannuation details and financial records, as well as any account details or passwords you'll need.

☐ **Notify their financial institutions:** Contact their bank, super fund and the taxation office to let them know they have died. They will ask you to provide documentation while they close their accounts and work through their processes (like the medical cause of death certificate and any documentation that proves you're the executor). Most banks have a deceased estates support line to guide you through the process. You'll need to notify and close any PayPal, cryptocurrency or other financial platform accounts.

☐ **Check for debts and liabilities:** Identify any outstanding loans, mortgages or credit card debts. Contact the lenders to discuss repayment or closure. If you don't have one, you might engage an accountant or solicitor to advise and help handle legal and tax obligations.

☐ **Close or transfer bills and subscriptions:** Make a list of and then systematically close or transfer any online accounts so that billing ceases. For example, this might include electricity, gas, phone, internet, streaming services and insurance (such as life, home, health, car and pet insurance).

☐ **Determine if the estate is subject to probate:** If it is, you'll need to initiate the probate process with a lawyer or the relevant state authority.

- ❑ **Claim entitlements:** Check for life insurance payouts, superannuation death benefits and any employer-provided benefits. File any paperwork needed.

- ❑ **Settle any immediate expenses:** Make sure you can cover funeral costs, medical bills or outstanding payments related to their care. Keep records of any payments you make if they need to be reimbursed.

- ❑ **Redirect their pension or government benefits:** Notify Centrelink, Veterans' Affairs or any other relevant agencies to stop payments and avoid overpaying.

- ❑ **Secure their assets:** Ensure that properties, vehicles and valuables are accounted for and properly managed.

Medical

- ❑ **Return medical equipment:** Contact equipment providers to return any equipment loaned, or organise to resell or dispose of anything you have purchased, such as wheelchairs, portable oxygen tanks or a hospital bed.

- ❑ **Safely dispose of medications:** Return any unused medications to your local pharmacy for disposal.

- ❑ **Cancel healthcare services:** Notify doctors, specialists and home care providers, as well as any upcoming allied health appointments (such as with a psychologist, acupuncturist or masseuse).

- ❑ **Request medical records if needed:** If required for legal or personal reasons, request copies of their medical records.

Digital/technological

- ❑ **Secure their email account:** You might need to access it while wrapping up their affairs, so make sure you have access and the right to do so. Close accounts as needed.

- ❑ **Manage social media accounts:** Decide whether to memorialise, deactivate or delete accounts on platforms like Facebook, Instagram and LinkedIn. You can add a legacy contact to a

Facebook account who can manage a memorialised account, or you can choose to have an account deleted if you'd prefer.

❑ **Close or transfer digital subscriptions:** Cancel online services like Netflix, Spotify, Apple Music and cloud storage accounts.

❑ **Work out what to do with their phone and computer:** Phones are very personal items these days, holding messages and often photographs and videos. Again, there's no rush. Take your time and seek help from someone tech-savvy if you need to back up the phone's contents to preserve sentimental files, or to wipe it so it can be used by someone else.

❑ **Redirect or close personal websites or blogs:** If they had a website or blog, determine what should happen to it. Consider any costs associated with this, such as domain name registration and site hosting.

Practical

❑ **Secure their home:** If they lived alone, ensure their property is locked, bills are paid and any pets are cared for. If they are renting, you'll need to let the rental agent know and work with them to vacate the property. Clean out the fridge before any sad, decaying vegetables can turn into science experiments.

❑ **Check for valuables and heirlooms:** Secure important or sentimental items before handling the rest of their stuff.

❑ **Sort personal belongings:** Decide what to keep, donate, sell or store. Allow time for family members to go through sentimental items. If you or others are remaining in the home, you might like to leave this until later when the dust has settled; if a home has to be sold (or they were living in a rental), this might be a big job. Accept help from the people saying, 'Let me know if there's anything I can do to help' here.

❑ **Redirect mail:** Set up mail redirection to prevent identity theft and ensure important documents aren't missed that arrive in the post.

❑ **Arrange property maintenance:** If their home needs to be sold or vacated, organise cleaning, maintenance and relevant inspections.

Social

❑ **Notify family and close friends:** Use a coordinated approach to inform key people respectfully. You can delegate this job to someone else or use a messaging platform like WhatsApp to save you telling the same story over and over again. Tell the people closest to them as thoughtfully and respectfully as you can—you don't want someone who cared for them deeply to find out about their death on a public Facebook post. Again, delegate the job to someone else if you need to—it's a big job, and you may not be thinking clearly. You also might not have the bandwidth to manage everyone else's reactions at this time. Take care of yourself.

❑ **Announce their passing:** Consider an obituary, social media post or funeral notice to communicate their passing more broadly, ensuring it's done thoughtfully. I announced Dad's death on my own channels but not on his, and wish I'd done a better job of that.

❑ **Coordinate funeral or memorial arrangements:** Work with a funeral director or plan a personal farewell, keeping their wishes in mind. Again, this is a big job with lots of little jobs, so let people help you. People love getting to contribute by taking over a task for an event like this: let them handle the flowers, the catering or something else for you. My best friend organised the printing of the take-home postcards for Dad's celebration of life. She wasn't able to be there in person but that was something she could do from afar, and one less thing for me to do.

❑ **Check guardianship arrangements:** If they had dependent children, family members or pets, ensure their care is arranged as per the will or legal agreements.

- ❑ **Inform employers and professional contacts:** If they were working, notify their employer and handle any final employment matters. If they were an employer, communicate sensitively with their team.
- ❑ **Contact clubs, memberships and charities:** Notify any organisations they were part of such as sports clubs, professional associations and volunteer groups, as well as any charities they had been supporting.

You've probably worked out by now that I have a tendency to distract myself with busyness when things are emotionally difficult. I'm a world-class doer, even (maybe especially) in crisis. It's probably a bit of a character flaw, but I hope you can reap the benefits by having somewhere to start here.

Before we go

Having someone die at home is an incredible gift, but it's hard—even for people with lots of experience.

Dr Shoshana Ungerleider is an American medical doctor and end-of-life practitioner who started a not-for-profit called End Well to transform how the world thinks about, talks about and plans for the end of life. She hosts a beautiful podcast called *Before We Go* about her experience taking care of her terminally ill father, and in it she says:

> **While I'd witnessed hundreds of deaths in a hospital setting, taking care of my own father in his home was so much more difficult than I thought it would be. We called that nurse advice line many times, even I did, and I'm an expert. The experience is really, really hard and no one is prepared for the stuff that comes up.**

All the practicality I covered earlier in this chapter doesn't and can't outweigh the monumental grief that moves in when someone you love dies. I don't know whether it's better or worse if a death is sudden or if you watch them suffer with illness but have time to say all the things. I suspect they are equally painful in different ways. Dad always said his mission in life was to live and die with ease and grace. I can't answer for him whether or not he achieved that, but I can confirm—outwardly at least—Dad died well. He never 'fought' or 'battled' his illness. He respected it, tried to coexist with it. Saw it as an unwelcome but accepted member of the family. He managed to die at home, surrounded by the people he loved. And I think there's an inordinate amount of grace in that.

On my part, as the observer, there are a few things I know for sure. The first is that pre-emptive loss—knowing someone is terminally ill—can feel like watching a wall of pain come towards you, sometimes for years. In the end, I was almost willing the universe to rip the Band-Aid off for his sake, even though for me it meant a life without Dad. There is only so much goodbye one person can take. The second is that it was the greatest privilege of my life to care for him in the same ways he once cared for me, down to what he ate, how he slept and the details of his bowel movements. I wouldn't give up a second of it, even the awful bits. The third thing I now know is that death is a great teacher. Being brave enough to explore and embrace it can enhance the quality and depth of our living.

The permanence of Dad's death still hasn't landed in my bones. While I started grieving as soon as he got his diagnosis, once he had actually died, when the tide had gone out, grief rushed in like a rising swell to take over. And there would come times I'd feel like I could almost drown in it.

CHAPTER 14

Flowers

'Stop here,' Dad says.

I pump the wheelchair brakes quickly in the hope my reaction speed is on point today. I don't want to miss the exact jasmine flower I know he has his eye on. I turn the wheelchair to face the low-hanging plant so Dad can carefully make his daily flower selection—a tradition I have come to love. When I am pushing him along, I watch people see us coming in the street. First, they see the wheelchair. Then, the man in it—looking too young to be pushed around. Next, the nasal tube delivering his oxygen gives away the fact that he is seriously ill. So far, the look on their face is of concern, sympathy or, sometimes, they either pretend not to or truly don't notice him at all, caught up with their important phone call, conversation or social media feed. If they do notice him, Dad's trusted green trilby hat is usually noticed next, followed by the flowers tucked neatly into the hat band. Once people notice these, their faces light up with the kind of big, toothy smile you only smile when something catches you off guard, like bumping into someone you love and haven't seen for ages.

In a conversation with one of his old girlfriends, I learn this practice isn't actually new for Dad—it's something he used to do back in the 1980s and has resurrected for this stage of his life. I ask him about the flowers and tell him I think it's nice to sprinkle a little joy for people. He tells me that—while it may bring joy to others—it brings the most joy to him. In that moment, I realise it's not actually about the flowers. It is the tiniest gesture to himself, others and the universe. A gesture of acknowledgement, mindfulness and gratitude. *I'm still here.*

Flowers can say a lot. They say, 'Thank you', 'I'm thinking of you', 'I love you' and 'I'm sorry'. It's ironic we send them when someone has died, given flowers die too. They are transient, just like us. Yet, we love real flowers much more than we do fake ones that last forever. There's something about their fleeting presence that makes them magical: that nature could throw those shapes and colours together with such reckless abandon, and that we can not only grow them but then cut the stems, curate them into an arrangement and buy them from the corner store to give to others. We send them to people who admire them for a few, precious days before they go in the garbage. When deep in grief, we're washing vases and working out the best way to fit dying bunches into the bin. For a moment, we hate those dead flowers. But then we get a fresh bunch and their intent lifts our spirit again momentarily, making us feel loved or appreciated or considered—a brief but welcome reprieve from grief we didn't choose.

'Grief is optional in this lifetime,' writes American grief expert David Kessler in his book *Finding Meaning: The Sixth Stage of Grief*, which he wrote as an extension of his work with his colleague and dear friend Elisabeth Kübler-Ross, the death and grief thought leader who developed the 'five stages of grief' model I mentioned in Chapter 13. 'Yes, it's true. You don't have to experience grief, but you can only avoid it by avoiding love. Love and grief are inexplicably intertwined.'

Perhaps for that reason, I can't think of many experiences that pack the punch of grief. Grief is a result of loss, and we all hate to lose. Before Dad, I'd been lucky enough to have limited experience with loss. Like most people my age, I'd lost grandparents and some beloved pets. I'd lost my beautiful mother-in-law and a few dear friends along the way. But I got to almost 40 with both parents, all my siblings, my partner and (praise be) my children, as well as the vast majority of my closest friends. I don't think it matters how much exposure you've had to grief or how 'uncomplicated' it is. I think grief is an entirely unique experience that doesn't play by any rules. Because grief requires professional care, in this chapter I'll lean on the experts a little harder, as well as share some of my personal insights with you.

Kübler-Ross's infamous 'stages' model gave us the five stages of denial, anger, bargaining, depression and acceptance, and now we consider them along with Kessler's more recently added meaning. We now understand that those 'stages' aren't really stages at all, and we don't move through them sequentially or in any sort of linear fashion. Kessler argues they were never intended as a map, rather as a range of experiences one might go through in the process of dying, but also in the process of grief.

When we think of grief, we often think of the grief associated with losing someone we love as perhaps the most intense grief of all. But I believe we're all grieving something. Our youth. Our children's youth. Our looks. Our fertility. Our first love. Our long-gone dog. What we thought life would/could/should have looked like at *insert age here*. Movies have hoodwinked our expectations of grief as commencing when our characters don head-to-toe black and attend a funeral. But when someone you love is sick, grief can start well before their life ends. There is grief that comes with navigating the cycle of hope when there are treatment options or when those options are working, and despair when there isn't or they aren't. It can be a rollercoaster, and not the fun kind.

My baseline of mild pessimism serves me well here. I'm not the grinch, crushing dreams and leaving crying babies in my wake, but I have found my worst-case-scenario thinking to be surprisingly effective in ensuring I get the most out of things, especially when it comes to time with the people I love. When Dad was given 6–12 months to live, I heard six at best and started quietly grieving him immediately. It wasn't intentional, but it's not an unwise strategy, even if you still have or want to hold on to hope. Hope and grief can coexist. But my glass-half-empty approach meant I acted with urgency and got every last drop out of the half-empty glass that had been put in front of me. It didn't protect me from or even prepare me for the pain of inevitable loss, but it meant I didn't dawdle. We immediately did the things — made the plans and actioned them. We didn't wait for an unpromised tomorrow.

I could feel my heart fracturing as it expanded to accommodate for the impending loss, but I figured it would kind of grow back around my grief when it eventually healed. Certainly, over time, my grief has changed. In the days and weeks after Dad's death, I launched hard into the doing — the mountain of organising and administrative tasks that come with wrapping up a life. Perhaps if I just kept moving, I could outrun the grief. Besides, I'd been grieving for two-and-a-half years by the time Dad died — surely now I could just move into a nicer, easier coexistence with the grief I'd already welcomed in. But in the following days and weeks, it's as though the dark cloud that had been quietly following me around got stormier. When weeks turned to months, the best way to describe my internal state was flat, like someone had taken a giant piece of shade cloth and put it up over my formerly sunny life. Everything looked different. Darker. Duller. More diffused.

I was participating in life: getting up, getting dressed and doing all the things. Working. Parenting. Exercising. Socialising. All without Dad. But my interactions felt crunchy, burdened with sadness. I couldn't muster enthusiasm for pretty much anything. Where my work had always felt purposeful, nothing felt worth it. My only reprieve was hitting the couch every night with my husband, where we'd eat too much and live vicariously through the characters on our TV screens, beautiful people with impossibly toned arms who shouted a lot and worked for the CIA/FBI/YMCA. I'd use food to push down the undercurrent of anxiety that overwhelming grief was going to rise up and hit me out of nowhere. This swell was nothing new; I've lived with an undercurrent of anxiety my whole life. But something about this felt different.

Am I depressed? I'd think. *Am I just exhausted and recovering from caring? Perhaps this is what middle age feels like? Maybe I'm deficient in something or — or — maybe I have a brain tumour. People's personalities can change when they have a …*

Standing in front of my wardrobe, grappling yet again with the rudimentary task of dressing myself for the day, it hit me in the face like a sad, wet fish.

Oh my god, this is grief.

I marvelled at my own naivety and then quietly burst out laughing at my brain, which had been doing its very important job of keeping me safe from harm. Grief was a threat, so of course it had been trying to come up with a million other reasons for my malaise. But there was a huge relief in calling it what it was—*I am grieving*. There was nothing wrong with me. Instead of beating myself up for my lack of chutzpah, my new motto became *gently, gently*. Gently on myself, gently on the world around me. Getting up, dressing myself and getting my kids to school—even after the bell had gone—was enough to achieve in a day. Anything beyond that was a bonus. And some days, I was firing on almost all cylinders. I could see glimpses of who I was and would be again in the future. But my grief was always with me.

Many of us think grief is deep sadness (which of course, sometimes it can be). But grief gets confused and isn't really a feeling or even an emotion. It's a response to loss, and a container that holds the emotions we experience as a result of that loss. In his podcast *Huberman Lab*, American neuroscientist and associate professor of neurobiology and ophthalmology at the Stanford University School of Medicine, Andrew Huberman describes grief as a process, one that has a beginning, middle and end. This doesn't really fit the idea that we don't move on from grief but rather carry it with us, even if it changes. But I think Huberman is referring to the physiological and psychological process the brain goes through in grief, rather than the emotional attachment to the loss we carry. And there's something comforting about knowing that we *will* move through the process, and we *can* redefine our relationship with both the person or thing we've lost, as well as with the grief itself.

Huberman refers to grief as a motivational state, because the brain areas associated with motivation, craving and pursuit are the same areas that researchers see on functional MRI machines as being active in grief. He says grief is akin to the feeling of there being something you really want but can't have.

Huberman says to think of being thirsty on a hot day, '… a glass of water is right in front of you … You so badly want to drink that water but no matter how intensely you want it and no matter how hard you try and reach it, it always shifts just outside your reach.'

Rather than quenching your thirst, you learn to live with this yearning, longing or desire that shapeshifts over time — but potentially not in a linear, decreasing fashion. Fresh grief can make you cry at the supermarket on a Tuesday, and 25-year-old grief can too. Old grief can feel like a dull ache, but you can feel the can't-put-your-finger-on-it pain at any stage. If the size of the grief is proportionate to the size of the love, the fact you carry it is a reflection of how much they meant to you, and there's something beautiful about that.

Once I knew what I was experiencing, I ran a bath, poured a cuppa and got in with my grief. And I stayed with it, even when it felt like I was trying to swim laps while wearing a thick winter jacket. Without oversimplifying the experience (and at risk of giving you a completely underwhelming analogy), grief is not dissimilar to scar tissue. Just like the Harriet Potter scar on my forehead, the emotional scar of losing Dad is still very much there. I can feel it and see it and there are no guarantees it won't get ripped open. But I have healed tremendously, in the way that only the human body — and heart — can. We are way more resilient than we give ourselves credit for.

I once heard someone say grief is like being given a heavy stone to carry around in your pocket. The stone never gets lighter, but you get stronger and better at carrying it around. In the beginning your grief can feel like it lives just under your skin, waiting for someone or something to press the grief button. But over time it becomes less raw, less visceral. A little deeper under the surface. The moments you feel like it could jump out from behind a corner and scare you get fewer and further between.

While I don't have the 'solution' to grief, I hope some of these observations can act as a wall to bounce your own enquiries off, and bring you comfort in some small way.

- **Grief is personal and unique.** You cannot compare, contrast or compress your grief to fit into anyone else's box. It is yours, even when it is shared.

- **Grief isn't always loud—it can be very, very quiet.** Like that feeling when you know you've forgotten something, but you can't work out what it is.

- **Grief doesn't work to project plans, timelines or finish lines.** Timelines with grief are arbitrary. You can't schedule your way out—you have to learn to live *with* the grief, not wait for it to be over.

- **Grief isn't contagious, but it can sure feel like it.** I isolated myself so my grief didn't rub off on others and—honestly—so I didn't have to perform life, which is what I felt like I was doing most of the time in the early days. That's okay. Lights, camera, action.

- **Grief can make you feel overwhelmed and empty at the same time.** It can feel like depression and anxiety and nausea and confusion and mania and deep sorrow, and it's likely that all of it is just grief.

- **This too shall pause.** I'd catch myself laughing or momentarily distracted from my grief. These periods of time started to slowly stretch out—the pause being some space where 'normal' seemed to live.

- **Grief doesn't come for a visit, it moves in.** Big meeting at work? You'll be taking along your colleague, grief. Dinner party for a friend? Set a place for grief. Heading on holidays? Pack a bag for your grief—it'll be going with you. But eventually, there will be more moments when you're okay than moments when you're not.

- **Welcome to a crappy but heartwarming club.** I've connected with so many people who have lost someone they love. Even if we have nothing else in common, there's an instant connection — a quiet respect that says, 'I know how you feel.' Find those people.

- **Little things, big things.** I girded my loins for each milestone the 'year of firsts' delivered — first birthdays without them, first Christmas, first anniversary — but those weren't the moments that floored me. It's the song in the supermarket, the order at the restaurant, the deep exhale after a long day when I'd love nothing more than to pick up the phone. It's a million little things that are actually big things, like Dad's laugh, his hugs and the way he'd always hold my hand. I'd give anything for one more hand-hold.

- **You're in as much control of your grief as you are of an election.** You can vote, but your candidate may not win on any given day. There is no point me hoping for 'good days' on the days I need to be switched on or perform or parent or be social — the grief does what the grief wants. My job is to hold on and ride the waves.

Being a container for others' grief

In the *Tao Te Ching*, Chinese philosopher Lao Tzu wrote that 'from caring comes courage'. The word courage comes from the Latin word 'cor', which means 'heart'. That makes sense, because the carers I know are the most courageous, wholehearted people I've ever met. They live and love with full and increased risk of grief, and they choose to care anyway. In our own grief, as well as the grief of others, there is certainly the need to be courageous. In the face of a terminal illness, you may have to watch the person you love not just lose their life but grieve for the life they will not have. You may have to watch them sideline their own grief to make room for the grief of others, who need them to be strong. And you might have to watch them grieve their relationship with you while they're still here. None of that is easy on the heart.

A year or so after I lost Dad, I had the opportunity to attend a deathwalker training with Zenith Virago, where we learned invaluable skills on how to walk people in our communities through death and all that comes with it. There, I learned we need to stop saying we can 'hold space' for someone's grief. Virago explained this gives us too much self-importance. It is not within our power to hold space for anyone—our only job is to witness their suffering and sit with them in it. She also taught us that our natural instinct to rush in with touch when someone is emotional, to pat their arm or come in for a hug, isn't necessarily what's best for them. If you know them really well it might be appropriate, but if they're even a tiny bit removed, give it a beat before you rush in. Let them sit with their suffering for a moment—it's a valid emotional response. Touch can disturb the emotional response and smother their experience. You'll see very quickly that they'll come out the other side of their tears, usually with a sigh, joke or comment, like 'it is what it is'. If you rush in, you may interrupt that loop for them. Simply be with their suffering. It is serving a purpose.

Canadian physician and trauma expert Dr Gabor Maté says we have two core needs: attachment and authenticity. For carers, our authenticity can go out the window when we park our own needs for others'. When people are relying on you, you can't authentically pause and take a load off—you keep going because you have to. You can't fall apart emotionally; you keep it together because you must. And your attachment? Well, that's threatened too. The person you're caring for might not be who they were: they may be grappling with their illness or injury, and as a result your relationship may change—for better or worse.

For people caring for their parents, you can experience a reversal of roles. Regardless of whether you had a top-notch childhood or one that left a bit to be desired, all of a sudden it is like you are the parent, they are the child and, in the face of losing them, you are preparing to detach from your most important attachment. To say that's complicated is putting it mildly, but if you have a decent support network and an even mediocre sense of self, you will get through it.

Talking about illness

Few of us communicate well at the best of times. We half-listen while we wait for our turn to speak, rehearsing what we'll say next regardless of what our conversation companion is sharing. As soon as our turn comes, we bring the attention back to ourselves, to our examples and our stories. We think this game of talk-tennis is how we should converse—you go talking about you, I go talking about me. But actively listening is the most important part of any conversation, especially with someone either grappling with their own mortality or a serious illness, or caring for someone who is. It can also be impossible to know what to say. In her book *Advice for Future Corpses (and Those Who Love Them)*, American essayist and palliative care educator Sallie Tisdale writes:

> Say: *This sounds very difficult.* Say: *I can tell how much thinking you've done about this matter.* Say: *Um-hmm. Tell me more.* Keep bringing your mind back to the present moment when you stray. Invite detail. Ask questions and make it clear that you want to know.

What Tisdale is saying is to keep the focus on them. It's not that your opinion isn't important, but it's their experience. Speak calmly and reflect back what you've heard to make sure they feel understood. While you can't 'hold space' for their grief, you can certainly bear witness to it, which can provide them with great comfort. Meet them where they're at, and if you don't know where they're at, ask them.

What to say (and not say) to someone who is grieving

It can be hard to know what to say to someone who has lost someone they love or is facing a difficult diagnosis. But there are a few things we shouldn't say, and it's worth being across them as well as having some alternatives.

- **Don't say** 'I'm sorry for your loss.' You might be deeply sorry for their loss, but when it's the 100th time they've heard this, it starts losing meaning.

- **Don't say** that what they're going through is 'unimaginable' or 'unbearable'—it's their reality and they have no choice but to bear it.
- **Don't tell them** the person they've lost had a 'good innings' if they've lived to an age you deem appropriate to die—that's not up to you to decide.
- **Don't say** 'Please let me know if there's anything I can do' because they don't know what day of the week it is, let alone what you can do for them.
- **Don't say** they 'battled' or 'lost' the fight. There are no winners or losers; people who die don't die because they didn't fight hard enough.
- And, **don't say nothing** out of fear of saying the wrong thing.

Instead, you could:

- **Acknowledge their pain:**
  - 'I can only imagine how hard this must be for you.'
  - 'I don't have the right words, but I want you to know I care.'
  - 'This must be so difficult. I'm here for you.'
  - 'This truly sucks. I'm really feeling for you.'
- **Offer specific support:**
  - 'I'd love to bring you a meal this week—would that be okay?'
  - 'I'm here to listen whenever you want to talk.'
  - 'I'd love to come and sit with you for a few hours on Thursday, would you like that?'
  - 'Can I help with [specific task, such as the school run/cleaning the house/walking the dog/doing the grocery shopping] to make things easier for you this week?'
  - 'Is there anyone I can communicate with for you to help lighten the load?'

- (If you are close to them) 'Would it be helpful if I took over some of the funeral tasks for you? I could help arrange transport/catering etc. Would that help?'
- **Share a memory (if it's appropriate):**
  - 'One thing I loved about [name] was [something meaningful].'
  - 'I'll always remember when [memory of the person]. They meant so much to so many people.'
- **Validate their experience:**
  - 'Take all the time you need, grief doesn't have a timeline. I'll be here when you're ready.'
  - 'There's no right way to grieve. I'm here for you in whatever way you need me to be.'

It's unlikely people in the acute stages of grief will remember who each bunch of flowers came from or who dropped a lasagne at their door on that day that felt like all the other days. But these gestures will help them feel loved and supported while they allocate their emotional resources to survival.

Remember too that you (or anyone) may be grieving someone you didn't have a good relationship with. Someone who wasn't supportive, or mistreated or even abused people. Relationships aren't always good or straightforward. Some people live complex lives and leave complex legacies. Bear in mind that the person you're speaking to might not be experiencing grief at all, they may be experiencing relief.

Robert A. Neimeyer is one of the world's most prolific grief researchers, as well as a clinician and professor of psychology at the University of Memphis. Many years ago, he posited the following in one of his research papers: 'A central process in grieving is the attempt to reaffirm or reconstruct a world of meaning that has been challenged by loss.'

I think that sentiment holds true today. Loss and resulting grief require us to rebuild, to find new meaning in a landscape without someone or something we thought would be there and now isn't. So, supporting someone as they re-orient themselves physically, emotionally and socially in the midst of loss is a generous act. They will come up for air eventually—your job is to be there with your hand outstretched for them to take when they're ready, while they try not to drown. Remember that grief doesn't have a timeline, so be patient. Send flowers three months later; make a lasagne when it's been six months and the calls and gifts have long stopped coming. Put a diary notification in your smartphone for the three-, six- and nine-month points as well as the one-year anniversary (and make that notification repeat annually forever).

Shoot them a text on those days, saying something like, 'No need to reply. Just wanted you to know I'm thinking of you and sending my love today.' The acknowledgement is the gift—for long after everyone else's life has gone back to normal, I can't tell you how much remembering means to the person who will never forget. On days like Father's or Mother's Day, text your friends who have lost those people and say you're thinking of them. Text them at Christmas or on any date you know would hold significance for them in the midst of having an empty space at the table. It only takes you 10 seconds to send, but it will mean the world to the person receiving it.

Talking to kids about illness and death

I am at a beach bar in Vanuatu, watching a fire show where people dance, twirl and blow fire like it won't burn their skin or singe their eyelashes. My four-year-old has lost the plot so she and I have escaped to the car to sit in relative safety. I assume she is overly tired being in a different timezone, and sugar-crashing after too much apple juice. Instead, she curls into my lap and sobs, saying only 'Papa' over and over again. I hold her as grief wracks her tiny body, an experience she can't understand let alone put words to. It is my strongest reminder yet that grief really is just love with no place to go.

Talking to kids about illness and death can be challenging, but there are a few things that can help. In this chapter, I've talked about grief in terms of both losing someone and the grief that comes with a poor diagnosis or prognosis, so the following has been written with both in mind.

- **Be honest and clear with simple, age-appropriate language:**
  - Use straightforward words: 'Grandpa was very sick, and his body stopped working.'
  - Avoid euphemisms like 'went to sleep'—they can be confusing and scary.
  - If the illness is ongoing, explain it in simple terms: 'Mum has an illness that makes her very tired, but the doctors are doing their best to help.'
  - Tailor the details to their age and maturity. Younger children may need concrete explanations, while older kids may have more complex concerns.
- **Follow their lead and encourage questions:**
  - Answer their questions honestly, but don't overload them with information. They'll ask for more if they want it.
  - Be prepared for repeated questions as they process the news in their own way.
  - Let them ask anything, even if it's hard. If you don't know the answer, it's okay to say, 'That's a really good question. I don't know, but we can find out together.'
  - If they ask tough questions (like 'Are you/they going to die?'), you might reassure them by saying something like: 'I'm doing my best to be here for a long time, and I'm taking really good care of myself.'
- **Validate and scaffold them:**
  - Let them know their feelings are valid: 'It's okay to feel sad, angry or not to feel sad sometimes.' It's okay to say if you're sad or worried too—it shows them it's okay for them to feel those things as well.
  - If the illness is affecting a parent or caregiver, remind them, 'You are still loved and cared for.'
  - Keep routines as normal as possible—structure helps kids feel secure. If anything about their current routine is likely to change, tell them.

- **Let them express grief in their own way:**
  - Some might cry, others might play as if nothing has happened—let their way be their way, you don't know what's going on internally.
  - Offer creative outlets like drawing, writing or making a memory box.
- **Explain what to expect:**
  - If a loved one is sick, explain changes they may see, such as the person starting to look different, being attached to medical equipment or needing more rest.
  - If there's a funeral or other ceremony, describe what will happen there and give them the choice to attend and participate.
- **Give them ways to stay connected:**
  - Talk about memories, look at pictures or create a ritual (like lighting a candle). The same daughter who was sobbing in Vanuatu recently lit three candles at dinner and—entirely unprompted—told me one was for my dad, one was for my mother-in-law and one was for my precious dog (who she never met).
  - Encourage them to write letters or make drawings for their loved one to cheer them up.
- **Use books and stories:**
  - Books about illness and death can help children understand and open up about their own feelings.
  - Do some research: there might be cartoons on YouTube or shows on TV you can watch together.
- **Let them know they're not alone:**
  - Share your own emotions in a way that's appropriate: 'I feel sad too, because I loved Grandma very much.'
  - Remind them they can talk to you whenever they need to.

When Dad died, my daughters were blissfully distracted by a Disney movie in the lounge room of Dad's apartment. After he had taken his final breaths, they came into the bedroom where his body lay to give him a kiss. My eldest went straight in for a hug, entirely unphased by his lifeless body and the crying adults around him. My youngest hung back, pulling on the edge of my tee shirt and motioning for me to crouch down so she could whisper something in my ear.

'Mum, has Papa gone to the angels now?' she asked, wide-eyed.

'Yes, sweetheart, he has,' I tearily told her. The 'going to the angels' narrative was a hangover from losing my mother-in-law years before, when my eldest was only two and my youngest was still in my belly. I don't know where it came from; perhaps I didn't know how to explain it in a way my toddler could understand, and in the moment that was the best I could do.

'But Mum, he's RIGHT THERE ...' my youngest said, motioning with her forehead towards Dad's body, careful and quiet so he wouldn't notice.

I quickly realised I'd done her a disservice — the language I'd used had been taken at face value by my very young child. I'd said he was 'going' but she was correct — he was indeed *right there*.

'Oh baby, his body is still there but his soul has gone to the angels,' I tearily explained. 'See? We opened the window so it could get out and fly away.'

She nodded as though she understood, though how could she possibly understand? But she leapt into the unknown anyway, walking forward and climbing up so she could hug and kiss him one more time. He would've loved it.

• • •

Looking back, I can see all the things I got right and so many things I got wrong. But care, loss and grief are never perfect. You will never get everything right. The mentor I'd sat with in the café two years prior, who'd told me I wouldn't walk away, had been absolutely right. I left nothing on the table, and my dedication to walking Dad out of this world made my grief uncomplicated—no regrets, nothing left unsaid. Just grief in its purest form for a man I loved beyond measure.

When I deliver a keynote speech, towards the end of my talk I always share a little of mine and Dad's story. He's there on my slides and in the room, and I get to share him with hundreds, sometimes thousands of people at once. In these moments, my grief nestles perfectly amid my purpose and doesn't trip me up. And other days I will sit frozen in time in my pyjamas, holding his ashes on my lap as I drink my morning coffee with tears streaming down my cheeks. Who knows what tomorrow will bring. Grief is running the show—I'm just along for the ride.

CHAPTER 15

The After Party

Dad and I are driving to pick up his coffin. We pull up to the cemetery, find who we're looking for and introduce ourselves. Two women have been waiting for us on a very hot day—Dad moves slowly, and we have been waylaid. They are kind and compassionate but, I suspect, a tiny bit pissed off. I understand and am deeply apologetic. Dad also understands and gives precisely zero f*cks. We open the back of Dad's truck and I can feel the women's eyes on us, probably wondering how we're going to lift the coffin into the back of the car and whether it will fit. I am strong but Dad is weak. While the coffin is made of environmentally friendly cardboard and relatively light, at a size 'large' to accommodate Dad's tall frame, it is awkward to manoeuvre due to its size and shape. And we are about to learn the hard way that the space we are trying to load it into is about two inches shorter than it needs to be. We struggle like bad removalists trying to fit a large couch down a tight stairwell, twisting and turning and trying again and again before agreeing to let the end simply hang out the back. We don't have far to go, we reason, assuring the women we will drive carefully and take full responsibility should the coffin escape from the back of the truck and find its way onto the road.

We make the short drive back to my house and unload the coffin into my garage until it's needed. I want to ask Dad how he's feeling but stop myself. I don't need to ask, I can only imagine. So we just park the coffin in the garage for me, my husband and small children to walk past multiple times a day as if it is a bicycle someone once bought on a whim.

Some weeks later, when we know the end is nearing, we arrange what Dad calls 'The Party Before the After Party'. His nearest and dearest are invited to gather at my house to eat, drink and decorate Dad's cardboard coffin while he is still with us. Showcasing his wicked sense of humour, Dad (whose name is Jack) decides it would be very funny if on the top of his coffin it says 'Jack in the Box', with a stamp that says 'Return to Sender'. I think he is hilarious and dying and therefore gets whatever he wants, so I engage a creative girlfriend who moonlights as a sign-maker to get to work on bringing his vision to life. She creates the design, sends it to us for approval, then comes over and measures, pencils and paints until the artwork is complete. Dad is as thrilled as one can be about the design of their coffin.

On the night of The Party Before the After Party, friends and family arrive at our house, a plate of food in hand to share with the group as Dad wanted. It is a warm night with a cool breeze, and we all sit wherever we can find space to eat and drink and be together. Throughout the evening, a few at a time, we move to the coffin and choose a small patch on which to leave our mark. Poems, illustrations, children's handprints, blessings and shells collected from beaches around the world adorn every square inch of coffin real estate, and we celebrate a life well lived with a potluck dinner and some 30 people who deeply care for Dad. We eat and laugh and decorate and take photographs and then we disperse. For most, it will be the last time they see Dad. Before I return the coffin to the funeral home's warehouse for its eventual use, I stick photographs of his favourite people on the inside of the lid, so he has something to look at when they put him inside.

We have a fairly well-trodden, historical formula for what happens when someone dies, at least in the wealthy, Western world. They pass, we pay; we cremate or bury with a service in a stuffy funeral home or, if we're lucky, somewhere a little nicer, then we drink too much alcohol at the wake because we're sad and want to feel happy again, even if it's artificial. For some, this is perfect. For others, I suspect it's what we do because it's what's been done. And, in the throes of grief, it is easier to follow the formula. But my limited experience has taught me that you want an end-of-life event to be a reflection of everything that came before. I couldn't imagine Dad going to a funeral, let alone having one. So I suppose the seed I'd like to plant with you in this chapter is that you can do pretty much anything you want to do, within the constraints of the law.

If you want to have a Party Before the After Party (sometimes known as a living wake), you can. If you want to have a traditional funeral, you can. And if you want to do nothing at all, you can. After Dad died, we didn't rush. A month later we threw him what he called 'The After Party'—a celebration of his life at the local bowls club where people could gather, connect and share. There was no official service. We had an Indigenous colleague of Dad's play the didgeridoo and welcome us to country, and my husband hosted the event so I could focus on not melting into a puddle. We sat in a circle and a few people said a few words. We shared a short section of the *Homecoming* video I'd put together for Dad to watch before he passed, at his request. There was no fancy catering, just a simple sausage sizzle, a cheese platter and some money on the bar. Our doula created the most beautiful altar, and people brought things to put on it that meant something to their relationship with Dad. My littlest brother contributed the footy he and Dad had spent hours kicking between them.

Before he died, Dad and I designed a postcard for people to take home with them at The After Party, with an image of him he loved and a message from him on the back. It read:

Greetings from Palermo, Italy (JOKING)*

Thank you for attending my after party! Sorry I couldn't be here, I'm off on life's greatest adventure. I am however leaving many loved ones behind to find their way, and hope you'll

all support them best you can through connecting, sharing stories and having some fun today and beyond.

Pagan blessings my beloved friends.

Jack

*I am not joking. It actually said '(JOKING)'.

I lost count of the number of people who came up to me and said they'd never thought about what they wanted at the end of their lives, but seeing it done differently had inspired them as to what's possible. I took it as a sign of a job well done, and a send-off Dad would've been proud of. If you are lucky, you will have the chance to design end-of-life arrangements with the person whose life is ending. If you don't, make it exactly what they would want — not what the people around them want. Think outside the jack-in-the-box. Would they want a burial? Or would they prefer to be cremated and have their ashes sprinkled somewhere in particular? Would they want a green burial or an eco-friendly coffin? Sure, they're not there to enjoy it — but we don't know they aren't watching.

One thing I would do differently if I had the chance is pour more energy into the ceremonial aspect of Dad's celebration of life. He just wanted it to be relaxed, so we made it relaxed. But while doing my deathwalker training, Zenith Virago taught us that 'a good ceremony can save you a lifetime of therapy'. I thought a ceremony was just a ritualistic event with a purpose, and that it simply needed to deliver against the wishes of the person you're saying goodbye to. But I now understand that a ceremony is also a powerful and poignant opportunity for the people left behind. A good celebrant (and ceremony) can take the bereaved on a meaningful, healing journey in a very short space of time, which can go a long way to helping or at least supporting the grief process. We did the best we could with what we knew at the time, but if I had my chance again I'd invest more time in getting that exactly right.

Managing your emotional state

Depending on how quickly you choose to have your ceremony (whatever that looks like), you may be deep in grief in the lead-up. You might be up to your neck in death admin or paralysed with emotional pain. There can be a confusing sense of both wanting the funeral or ceremony to be over and also knowing that life will be very different once it is. You might feel ready or not ready. Anxious or calm. Content or aggravated. Angry or enlightened. Devastated or numb. You might be in shock if the death was sudden or unexpected, even though the very nature of being alive should teach us that we can all expect death to come one day. Regardless, it's likely you'll need to carefully manage your emotional state.

Our energy is affected by many things: our physical health, how we've been eating (well, not well or at all), how we've been sleeping and how we're faring emotionally. It is a delicate balance on our best days, and a slog on our worst. You may feel like you are crawling through mud, which is unfortunate given there will be a lot of demands on you in the lead-up. You'll need to be protective of your energy during this time; you may need to get someone you trust to be your 'bouncer' — getting others to go through them if they want to get to you. They can act as a buffer or filter to ensure that what (and who) comes to you is absolutely necessary, allowing you to focus your energy and attention on your grief and healing.

On the day, everyone will want a piece of you. People will say the same things over and over again — usually well-intentioned but poorly understood platitudes that are said when we don't know what else to say. You may feel as though you are performing, playing the role of a person attending a ceremony for someone they love. You may feel nervous, and nervous energy is exhausting. Nervous energy makes you feel like you have been doing hill sprints for hours, or running from a vicious cat just to fall into a deep hole. All of that is okay. Try to eat something semi-healthy. Drink some water. Don't drink too much alcohol. Lean on someone, hard. Listen to your body and your mind. Be present. Breathe. Take your time. If there was ever a time to ask for what you need, this is it.

Afterwards, you might feel empty. You've been in motion for some time, maybe a long time, and now you might feel suspended in mid-air like the picture on the TV is frozen. Run a bath. Pour a cuppa. Get some biscuits. Invite a friend over or be alone. Distract yourself with terrible TV. The world will still be there when you're ready to climb out.

After The After Party: Ashes to ashes, beach to beach

Dad had requested we scatter his ashes at the beach near where he grew up, not too far from home but somewhere we'd rarely go with him or otherwise. We're spoiled for beaches in Western Australia, so those of us who live coastally can usually have a selection of world-class beaches within a fairly short drive of our door. As Dad's one-year anniversary approached, I tried wrapping my head around how we'd memorialise the milestone with a catch up and a scatter at his requested place, and couldn't for the life of me see it in my mind. I was imagining my elderly grandparents tottering across the fairly lengthy stretch of sand before you get to the water. Us hoiking up the legs of our pants (would we be wearing pants? And would we indeed hoik them or just let them get wet?). Us all moving swiftly past the many swimmers at one of the busiest beaches in Perth (cheers Dad) trying to look innocent and like we weren't about to make them breaststroke through human remains. I tried to arrange dates and times and nothing felt right or worked for everyone, so I gave up momentarily and figured future me would at some stage figure out the exact right timing to honour Dad's wishes.

Some time later, I was listening to a podcast interview with death doula and educator Alua Arthur (who I introduced you to in Chapter 13). She was sharing the story of a woman who had nursed her husband, and at his celebration of life she had taken 100 of those old film canisters, filled them with his ashes and put them on a table for people to take home with them. If you're under the age of 30 and have no idea what I'm talking about, we used to have to put a roll of film into a camera and then, when it was finished, physically take it to a bricks-and-mortar store to have it developed and ... never mind. Enjoy your cloud. Anyway, this woman divided her husband's ashes into these canisters and offered anyone to take one if they felt called to. The condition was that if they chose to take one, they had to scatter his ashes somewhere, take a photograph of the place and write her a letter explaining why they chose that place and what it meant to them, or him, or them together.

What she ended up with was many letters and photographs, stories that she knew and others she didn't. And he ended up in 100 different places, so that — rather than there being one place for her to visit him in future — there were many. I love the idea of Dad being all around me rather than scattered in one place, even if his chosen ocean would carry him elsewhere. So, I hedged my bets. We split his ashes in half and then split one half into portions for the people he loved most. With the unportioned half we will eventually do as he requested, scattering them at his childhood beach. We will totter, hoik and scatter and it will be beautiful. But with our own portions we will each choose our own place, scattering them somewhere that means something to us and then reporting back so our place can mean something to everyone else too.

It's not exactly what he asked for, but I think he trusted me to make that call and I know he'd be quietly chuffed that we all had the chance to make a powerful ritual of our own. I'm proud of how we approached Dad's death and the ceremonies that came with it. We did it his way and our way. It may not be right for anyone else, but it was right for us. And that's all it ever has to be.

CHAPTER 16

Places

After Dad was diagnosed, for a long time you might not have known he was sick. He didn't really look like a sick person, outside of when he turned green from chemo. He didn't behave like a sick person, and only the people close to him could tell he wasn't himself. To others, I suppose he just seemed like a tall, handsome, sometimes grumpy man. He almost never wallowed, but rather did his best to juice every drop out of whatever was left of his life. We ate out for breakfast on a Tuesday because we could, went to the beach just because, took road trips and went camping — all things someone who wasn't dying (or watching someone die) might take for granted.

At night, Dad's favourite thing to do became to sit down with whoever was there so we could lose ourselves in a TV series. We all had our own show with him, so he would have four or five on the go at any one time. We'd eat dinner and then settle onto the couch or open the laptop on his bed to tuck into our show with his favourite dessert — vanilla ice cream with Maltesers on top. The ice cream thing was new for Dad — I don't remember him ever really having a sweet tooth. Long gone was his attempt to not feed his cancer with sugar, replaced with what I imagine was a desire to feed his joy instead. After all, YOLO. His tastebuds were never the same after chemo, so perhaps the intensity of the cold and sweet was enough to make them feel something again. I'm still not sure how I didn't end up the size of a house during this period of time, always saying yes given I didn't know how many more yeses I'd get to say. I guess grief does funny things to people's eating habits and I was probably running on empty for much of the day, which perhaps counterbalanced the daily ice cream binge.

Other people's stories kept us entertained and distracted from our own. We'd sit or lay side-by-side, occasionally piping up if one of us had a question, felt called to make a comment or needed a fresh cup of tea. I suspect that if someone counted, we'd have clocked millions of cups of tea between us. Me weak and black during the day, herbal at night. Him weak, black and with a generous teaspoon of honey, day or night. One of his and my favourite shows was *1883*, a prequel to the hit series *Yellowstone*, which was, of course, one of the best series of all time (fight me). *1883* is a cowboys and Native Americans wagon-trail drama based on a family's journey from Tennessee to Montana in pursuit of a better life. One of the hero characters, Elsa, is a young cowgirl who has just lost her first love to a bow and arrow and is, understandably, devastated. In a pivotal scene, one of the elder cowboy leaders, Shea, tells her:

When you love somebody, you trade souls with them. They get a piece of yours and you get a piece of theirs. But when your love dies, a little piece of you dies with them. That's why it hurts so bad.

He goes on to explain that the little piece of his soul was still inside her, and that she could carry him around with her so he would see the world through her eyes. Kind of like when a parent lifts a child onto their shoulders so they can see better. I used to love when Dad would put me on his shoulders. Being up there felt like being on top of the world. I felt safe from everything, like no one could catch me even if they wanted to. He carried me on his shoulders, but he also just lifted me up in general. Dad invested so much time in me as a kid.

Apparently, my birth inspired him to briefly study child psychology, work in education and learn everything he could about how to turn me into a great person.

He didn't have much, but he used what he did have to great effect. He taught me to count using the letterboxes on our street. To multiply using hundreds of tiny Australian flag toothpicks that he grouped into different amounts to illustrate the concept of multiplication. And we were frequent flyers at the local library, where we would step inside the worlds of Roald Dahl, Enid Blyton and Dr Seuss. One of my favourite Dr Seuss stories was *Oh, the Places You'll Go*. I loved Seuss's playful, nonsensical language, but also that the story seemed to mean something. I didn't know it, but that book was my first foray into personal development with its strong message of being open to where life takes you, strapping in for the lows and not letting yourself get lost in the highs. I didn't know what any of it meant, but I wanted whatever it was. I wanted to *go* to those *places*.

Turns out, my life would indeed take me places. Exciting places, like the media, fancy parties and Italy. It would also take me to scary places. Dark places. Places that make me wonder how I'm still here at all. Now, I can look back and see that — so far — my life has followed the same ups-and-downs pattern as everyone else's, just like in *Oh, the Places You'll Go*. Mine are uniquely mine, as Dad's were uniquely Dad's, as yours are uniquely yours. But it's our people that carry us through them, there to soften the blows and cheer the highs. We are never walking alone.

I don't know how it came about, but somewhere along the way Dad and I decided we were going to get matching tattoos. When Dad went into hospice I thought perhaps we'd missed the boat, and I didn't want to put any pressure on him by raising it. It simply wasn't a priority. Sitting in the sunshine at the courtyard table of his hospice room one day, on the phone advocating for something Dad needed and tapping away on my laptop, Dad came out with a pen and grabbed my arm. He wrote TATTOOS on my wrist, the very best kind of to-do to add to my list. So I made the appointment and a couple of days later we drove to a local tattoo artist, who carefully put together a design and got the gun ready to go. *Oh, the Places We'll Go* was inked carefully onto my wrist and his forearm, a little part of him to live on on me, and a little part of me to accompany him to the one place I couldn't go.

Make it meaningful

We are a meaning-making species, storytellers that use narrative to make sense of the world around us. When we lose someone we love, or someone gets a poor diagnosis, we want to understand the meaning behind it. Why this? Why now? Why them? Why me? I suspect this is the reason 'meaning' has been added as the sixth stage of grief. Not because we'll always know why, but because we can try to get to a place where we can choose what meaning we attach to it, and see any good that comes out of a bad deal.

On the way, the world will keep moving whether we like it or not. I couldn't wait to get the infamous 'year of firsts' over and done with after Dad died. Not because the important days feel heaviest with grief — I miss him most in the quiet moments, the ones with no cake that are not marked on the calendar — but because there is pressure on the big days to be significant. In some ways we were lucky that in the months following Dad's passing we had a baptism of fire when it came to firsts. The day after Dad passed was my littlest brother's 18th birthday. Five days later was Dad's 69th birthday, followed by Christmas and then my 40th — all within weeks of losing him. We braced and planned and compensated and tried to celebrate our way through those first few months, fuelled by the sort of adrenaline that only comes from having just lost one of your favourite people in the entire world. It felt like running downhill while bawling your eyes out.

Of course, there is something about days like Father's Day for someone without their dad or Mother's Day without their mum. If it were a hallmark card, the front would read:

A day all about you, without you.

Those days are hard; hold the people who need support steady on them.

For some, meaning is easy to find. For others, it's a harder job. But when we try to attach too much purpose or meaning to something, we can miss the very thing we're looking for. We can try too hard to make it meaningful, rather than allowing the meaning to show itself and find us. Perhaps, it's not about the cake but about the smell of candles that have just been blown out. Not about the gathering, but about the one quiet conversation you had in the corner. Not about the gift, but about the three last words in the card. If we are too focused on finding meaning, we can lose it altogether. How we choose to honour them moving forward should be as personal and unique as everything else we've brought to the experience of loving and losing them. On the big days, we can do everything or nothing or something in between, as long as it holds meaning to us.

Legacy

Dad's legacy was revealed when he got sick — it is us. His five children. It is my older sister's whip-smart brain and her goofy, dark sense of humour. My little brother's second-guessing of himself, even though he is already everything he needs to be. My younger sister's ability to question what she is told, and her passion for funny tee shirts. And my youngest brother's long limbs and big heart. And me? I haven't met all the ways his legacy lives in me yet. I hope, at the very least, it is in my generosity of spirit. When I was little, Dad used to do something we called num-nums. He'd put his face on my neck, between my jaw and shoulder, and say 'num-num-num', the humming sound vibrating through his prickly beard and making me squeal with laughter. I loved it, and — even though I am beard-less so it's less effective — have adopted it with my own children. They too squeal with delight and it's one of the things they want 'again, again, again' even though it occasionally makes my youngest wet her pants. Watching us play one day, Dad told me how proud he was of the mum I had turned out to be. He said I had the power of the num-num, and it was one of the greatest compliments I have ever received. Maybe he lives on in the num-nums.

I think we all spend our lives searching for our 'thing'. Our purpose, our justification for existence — the thing that makes us throw off the bed covers and leap out of bed in the morning. I know Dad did, and I don't know that he ever found it. But now I think I can see that Dad's purpose was to be the best dad he could be, which is a pretty exceptional goal. It's the reason he religiously carved out time for a weekly call with my big sister overseas. The reason he let my curious brother cut the fish they'd catch open so he could see what was inside, even though it made Dad squeamish. The reason he came to my little sister's netball games and littlest brother's footy games, even when he was too sick to be there. And the reason that — no matter where he was living — he always, always made room for us, even if it was just a mattress on the floor. We were, as the French would say, his *raison d'être*: his reason for being.

I too have spent a long time trying to find 'my thing'. The people who inspire me seem to go all-in on something they become known for, and I have been desperate to find the thing I would become known for. I would try ideas on and sometimes wear them for a while, but eventually decide I didn't like the colour or the fit after all. Like a giant puzzle, though, slowly my purpose has started to come together.

My purpose is to inspire people to take better care of themselves and each other, in the hope it delivers more time with the people we love most.

Health and care are the most powerful levers we have to do that with, and right now my job is to teach and guide people to use those levers to maximum effect. Tomorrow, someone might knock my puzzle off the table and I'll have to pick the pieces up and start putting it together again. But for now, I know I am incredibly lucky that my purpose, passion and career are intertwined. I have spent a long time asking health questions, then my care experience with Dad answered some, raised more and lit my purpose on fire. For many people, this convenient alchemy is not the case. You might be one of the many,

many people currently doing a soul-crushing job to pay the bills. It's not your purpose but it's serving *a* purpose. Your time will come.

I think what tripped me — trips us — up is this search for our one thing, our one purpose. Now I understand that purpose is not one thing but what drives us to do many things. Your purpose may be to be a great parent or daughter or friend. It may be to change people's lives in little or big ways. It may be to leave the world a better place than you found it. It may be to make one person's life better every day. None of those purposes require you to know 'your thing'. They just require you to lean into and follow the breadcrumbs of what feels good. I know first-hand that those breadcrumbs can lead you to places that feel like they have been waiting for you to arrive. And, I wonder if maybe, just maybe, our *people* are our purpose.

I believe death is the most powerful filter we have for living a richer, more grateful life. It changes you, but it changes nothing around you. I had front row seats to Dad's death *and* I still swear, struggle and scream when I catch my toe on the edge of the couch. But I don't sweat the small stuff (as much). After going through the worst thing, small grievances have become mere nuisances that ruffle my feathers much less than they once did. These days, my anxiety comes not from lack of achievement, but from not getting as much out of my life as humanly possible. I take every opportunity but don't obsess over hunting them down. I stop people in the street to tell them they have a beautiful face. As if it is law, I never say no to cake. I pat all the dogs. And if I get the chance to hug a stranger, I take it every time. My appetite for life is voracious now, and there's very little I take for granted.

The most powerful thing we have to give each other is our time. Dad gave me his when I was a baby and a child, and I gave him mine. When I grew into a young, semi-selfish adult, I gave all my time to other things I deemed more important. Dad was patiently waiting in the wings. Our parents always are, until they aren't. As soon as I knew time was limited, I gave Dad my time again. And it was, without a doubt, the most powerful and meaningful time of my life.

I remember reading once that time is the only currency we spend without ever knowing our balance, so we should use it wisely. Our time is like a melting ice cube; we'll never have more than we do right now. What I know is that caring for someone in their darkest hour is perhaps the richest experience you'll ever have using time you'll never get back. Don't get me wrong, it's the hardest of hard. Some days you'd give anything to tap out. But when you pack the experience away physically, mentally and emotionally afterwards, you'll know you had a direct impact on someone's life during their toughest time. And I don't know if there's any better return on investment than that.

The fact we get to live at all is a small miracle. To get to the end, whenever that is, in a body riddled with evidence of the trees we climbed and dance floors we lit up is an unfathomable gift. Like the tattoo on my wrist, I will carry Dad with me as I continue chasing my dreams and falling down along the way. And I know he is cheering me on, putting Band-Aids on my scraped knees and lifting me onto his shoulders so I can check out the view from the best seat in the house.

Epilogue: Air

There's a little island off the coast of where I live called Wadjemup. It means 'place of spirits' in Noongar, our Indigenous language. It's a beautiful island with a fairly ugly history. For many years, the island was used as an Aboriginal jail for men and boys, with some 4000 prisoners held there who were put to work building the prison and settlement infrastructure. They were poorly treated and many died, buried in unmarked graves. That history wasn't advertised for a long time, the island instead choosing to go by Rottnest—the name given to it by Dutch explorer Willem de Vlamingh, who thought the native marsupials—quokkas—were giant rats (Rottnest = 'rats' nest' in Dutch).

Families and holiday-makers took their boats, rode their bikes and rolled out their towels for decades before they knew. My family was no different, and it wasn't until well into adulthood that I started to cotton on, Dad thoughtfully educating me as he always did. Until then, I'd been like any other kid—enjoying our beloved 'Rotto' for its lack of cars and abundance of freedom as well as the doughnuts from the bakery, which are exceptional.

In the middle of the island is a series of salt lakes, which occupy a big chunk of the internal land area. The water in them is saltier than the sea but the surrounding plant life has adapted, creating a unique wetland habitat that's ripe for quiet reflection and feels a bit apocalyptic. It's unlike anywhere else in the world I've been. Beautiful, but harsh.

My mum grew up Catholic and while Dad was spiritual, he wasn't religious. I suspect due to his strong views at the time, Dad won the battle of me not being baptised. Instead, when I was a baby, Dad took me to a particular part of the Wadjemup salt lakes where he performed his own baptism. Just him, me and some very salty water. I don't know what he said but I know it meant something to him and now it means something to me.

Wadjemup was a special place for us, and even when he got really sick, he still braved the ferry to come over and join me, my husband and our girls for one last time. He wasn't willing to give up even one precious day with us, and those are the times I will cherish always. On that trip I had this grand vision of the two of us swimming together in the bluest of blue Indian Ocean, holding hands, washing away some of the toll that the last few years had taken on us in this magical place where he once baptised me. But on the day it was stormy and grey, and while I'd have braved the rain in a heartbeat, his body was no longer up to swimming in the cold.

More than a year later, my little family and I are on the ferry to Wadjemup. I stare at the horizon in an attempt to stave off my sea-sickness, which is inconveniently getting worse as I get older. In my bag is my towel, swimmers, hat, bottle of water, the million snacks you need to travel with children and a jalapeño jar holding my portion of Dad's ashes. The ferry docks and we step off the boat, grabbing our bikes from one of the deckhands and walking them along the jetty as is the rule. When we get to the end, we hop on and ride past the settlement, with its delicious doughnuts and opportunistic quokkas. We ride past the hotel (which was once the prison) and circle around the back to the salt lakes. I don't know the exact spot but I know the general vicinity, so we pull up there and lean our bikes against a nearby fence. The harsh ground cover crunches beneath our feet as we make our way over to the water's edge, where I carefully retrieve the jar from my bag. My youngest and I kiss the jar's lid, then we take it off—me saying a silent prayer a gust of wind doesn't pick the ashes up and throw them in our faces. My daughter carefully pours some out, instinctively saying, 'I love you Papa,' as she does. I realise I should have thought of something to say too, but instead I simply say:

'I love you Dad. I was so lucky to get to care for you. Thank you for being my person.'

My daughter hands me the jar and I tip the rest out slowly. The ashes dance on the breeze before floating down to land briefly on top of the water. For a moment, the water looks unsure whether to accept the ashes, then changes its mind and embraces them instead. I search them for meaning like those tea-leaf readings I've seen in the movies in the hope they give me a message from Dad. Nothing. I lean over, hoping to see my reflection or ideally Dad's, like Simba did with Mufasa in *The Lion King*. Still nothing. I dip my fingers into the ash-water, splashing some onto my cheeks and the back of my neck. Then I dip them again and place a perfect, salty T-shape on my five-year-old's forehead, continuing the ritual for the next generation. Without prompting, she reaches down, dips her hand into the water and then does the same to me and my heart feels like it may explode.

Afterwards, we ride slowly towards Pinky Beach. At the lighthouse we park the bikes and kick our shoes off, walking the short, sandy path to the ocean. It is the kind of day I wanted on that last trip with Dad. The air is still but not heavy, the sun warm but not scorching. The bay isn't perfectly calm but the waves are playful, water aqua blue and sand the sort of white other countries pay millions of dollars to import. I step into my swimmers with just enough dignity to avoid flashing my fellow beach-goers and just enough humility to not care if I do. Free of my belongings, I step towards the shore, my toes quickly finding the cool water. I take my time, stopping to let my body acclimatise to the temperature. Then, I dive in. The waves roll me around like I am dough. Then, I come up for air. I breathe it into all the spaces that have been holding their breath, waiting for life to begin again.

Floating on my back, I think about Dad's relationship with the ocean. Growing up, he loved the beach. He was a keen snorkeller and spearfisher for many years, spending much of his time at the beach as a youth. Over his lifetime he would dedicate so much to the ocean, not just with the Save Ningaloo campaign but through the Australian Marine Conservation Society, the local branch of which he ran for a while, and Ocean Care Day, a day that was his brainchild dedicated to teaching us all to take better care of the ocean. In perhaps my first ever speaking gig, he recruited a young me to dress up as a mermaid, get dropped off a boat just offshore and swim in, where he carried me onto the sand to deliver a speech to kids about why we should look after the ocean. Apparently the kids were losing their minds, and I was somewhat convincing as a maid of the mer.

As I would learn in one of our interviews, as he got older Dad's fear of the ocean—and particularly of sharks—had grown steadily. He told me:

'I like spending time near it, walking along the edge of it and occasionally being in it but it scares the crap out of me.'

It's not unlike how many of us approach life, to be honest. Going all in scares us. There are sharks in there that could come and take us any time. There are big sharks like disease, death, loss and grief. Little sharks like rejection, disappointment and heartbreak. So, we tiptoe around the edge. Maybe go in up to our knees. Surely the sharks can't get us there. But when we really go in, completely submerge, the water wraps itself around the fear and pacifies it. We are reminded that we won't sink, because we can swim. We can swim and survive, even though there are sharks.

Cool and cleansed, I get out and sit on the beach. The breeze has picked up now and it dances around me, flicking grains of sand that stick to my skin. Dad always said that when you're heartbroken you need to allow yourself to really feel it, to let the wind blow through the space where your heart used to be. So I close my eyes, take a deep breath in and let the breeze blow through me, a tear rolling down my cheek. I think about the fact that even with his fear of sharks, Dad kept getting in. Having a go. Coaching us through our fears of the same things, while quietly harbouring his own. I guess that's the thing about being Next of Kin, isn't it? We are brave for each other, especially when one of us can't be. All around me I can hear people: kids playing with parents, friends catching up, Next of Kin spending precious time together. The sounds make me happy.

All science and history have ever done is try to buy us more time. We are living longer than ever and still life is unfairly short. While we know the mortality rate of life is 100 per cent, in a strange way, a poor prognosis is a gift. It starts a countdown you didn't otherwise have and makes you aware of it, and you can choose to wallow in the injustice of the prospect of having less time, or you can make the most of the time you have. Of course, being dealt a bad hand doesn't mean life will play by our rules; it still won't go the way we want it to sometimes. Relationships end. Tires go flat. Flights get cancelled. Babies don't sleep. Plans don't go to plan. We don't get the job. We fight with our friend. We stuff up the meeting. We fail the test. And right beside us the whole beautiful, messy, complex, infuriating way, is our Next of Kin.

While he's no longer here with me, when I need Dad I can find him. I can find him in the ocean, in bowls of noodles, in the pink and grey galahs that surround my home. In sarongs and deep laughs and cups of black tea with honey. In second breakfasts, flowers in hats, soup spoons and coins under the couch cushions. I am not the first person to lose someone I love, nor will I be the last. That is why this book exists: to encourage you to care if you are given the chance. When someone you love needs you, step up. It'll be one of the most worthwhile things you'll ever have the privilege of doing, and it's time you'll forever be grateful for when you're swimming without them.

Given we never know when our time will be up, we'd best make the most of what we've got—and all we've really got is today. So, don't wait. Tell the person you love their face. Eat the cake. Pat the dog. Hug the stranger. Call your dad. Dance all night. Book the ticket. Take the class. Say you're sorry. Start again. Start late. Always swim. Paint it green. Cut it off. Dye it pink. If you don't like it, you can always change it back.

Of all the wisdoms I've shared here, it's only fair I give the last word to Dad. He always drove me to and picked me up from the airport. It was kind of our thing. I'll never forget walking through the airport with him one day; we were talking about his diagnosis and the bittersweet beauty it had delivered—more time together—and he turned to me and said:

'It's all just a glorious tragedy, isn't it?'

And he was right, it is. Life *is* a glorious tragedy. That's what makes it so worthwhile.

Don't go it alone. To join the kiin community and access a first-of-its-kind club for carers focused on connection, guidance and education, scan the QR code below.

Acknowledgements

Ryan AKA RyBaby. Even though I've managed to pour 70 000+ words into this, I can't find the right ones to express how grateful I am for you. Thank you for the endless cups of coffee delivered to my desk, giving me the time and space needed to write this and for not skipping a beat through the entire experience of caring for and losing Dad. You stepped up in ways I never would've even known to ask for, let alone expected. You've felt like home from the very beginning, and 10+ years in lucky doesn't begin to describe how I feel getting to be yours. I'm sorry for biffing everything and always making us late, and also sorry to say both will probably continue for life. Thanks for loving me anyway.

My babies. Neither of you are babies any more, but in the wise words of Mariah, you'll always be my baby(ies). That will make sense when you're older. For now, please know that while it might sometimes feel like my laptop is the love of my life, that title fairly and squarely sits with the two of you. One day you might have to do everything in this book for me, so it is for you as much as it is for everyone else. Thank you for your cuddles, kindness and wonder. You are my favourite people.

Mum. I am eternally grateful to have been birthed by the most generous person I know. From the dance floor to the chocolate aisle and everything in between, there's very few people I like spending time with as much as I do you. Also, you're the only parent I have left so you have no choice but to stick around now okay? Deal. I love you.

My Dad siblings. I am so, so glad we have Dad in common. I hope you know deep in your bones how much he adored you, and I'm putting it in print so you never forget. [P.S: Finally the kettle is mine!]. V: What I wouldn't give for a teleportation machine. I can't wait for the day we're together again. E: If Dad was here, and I know he is, he'd say; go get 'em girl. I won't say the world is your oyster because you hate oysters, just know I am so proud of you and behind you every step of the way. A: I can't wait for you to see just how powerful you are and take a big, giant bite out of this world. It's waiting for you. And if it sucks, we'll be right here waiting for you. Promise. C: We're not supposed to have favourites but you're probably mine (don't tell the others). Your maturity throughout losing Dad blew me away, and now you've gone through one of the toughest things so early, the rest will be a breeze. I love you.

Kylie. Thank you for raising me, protecting me and making me laugh harder than anyone else on Earth. You'll always be Kylie Minogue to me.

Nan. I can't imagine how painful it was for you to lose your baby. Your strength and grace during that time was beautiful to watch. He adored you, and I adore you. We all do. Thank you for being the matriarch you are and always modelling big heart, big humour and prioritising family over all else.

Sohalia. I don't know what I did to deserve you but holy hell am I glad I did it. You were my saving grace during these years. You got the best and worst of Dad and loved him anyway—thank you for giving so much of yourself to our experience, I know it left its mark on you, literally and figuratively. I hope we imprinted on your heart as much as you did on ours, and as much as I know you did on Dad's.

My girl gang. You know who you are. For cheering me on, entertaining my children, dropping meals, checking on me for proof of life and never getting annoyed that I have an average turnaround time of four days on messages if I respond at all—thank you. You are the funniest, kindest, best people on the planet and I can't believe you're my friends.

Jen. I'll never, ever get over you capturing Dad for me so I could have a little piece of him on my 40th birthday. The way you love me is so genuine and unconditional, it always has been—even back when I was a professional menace. Also, I'm not sorry for rubbing John's legs before he died. I stand by the fact he liked it.

Meera, James and my Byron godfamily. *Next of Kin* is a book about family, and there is no family I feel more a part of than yours. Thank you for making room for me from the very beginning, for including me and for so generously giving me the space I return to like a homing pigeon more often than you'd probably like. I am forever grateful for you.

The women (and men) who loved Dad. Each and every one of you completed Dad in some way. I know he was probably infuriating to be in a relationship with at times, but you all persisted because you knew—you know—he was also magic. Thank you for making him feel loved, scaffolding him when he needed it and for raising his children, whether they were yours or not. You are ~~good~~ great people. And especially to Eve, who loved Dad at the end when it would've been hardest of all. Thank you.

Lee. You need a special mention. Thank you for your support while Dad was sick and in the aftermath. I can't tell you how much it meant having you in my corner. My siblings are lucky to have you, and so am I. Thank you.

Zenith. How fortunate am I to be able to tap into one of the wisest, worldliest souls on the planet on such an important topic. Thank you for your generosity—with your time, with your wisdom and with your guidance. I am eternally grateful for you.

The Wiley team. Whether you acquired, shaped, read, polished, laid out, project managed, designed, marketed or sold this book; as soon as I met you, I knew I had found my publisher. Thank you for believing in this and for being invested in getting it right every step of the way. I feel so lucky to get to work with you. Jordon—thank you for getting it. I adore you. Kerry—thank you for your thoughtful polishes, you made the editing process disturbingly enjoyable.

Chris—thank you for not only keeping the train on the tracks but doing it with heart. Renee—marketing is not my strong suit, but you make it easy and fun. Thank you. And to the sales team; if this book is a success it will be because of you. Thank you for getting this into the hands of the so many who need it.

Sim and the TLS talent team. Simmy, you never, ever gave up on this project and I am eternally grateful. While I am the author, you are always the one who knows exactly what to say … just know I have a special place in my heart reserved for you and it's right next to the snacks, which you know is saying a lot.

My interviewees. To the exceptional humans who so generously gave up their time and wisdom to inform this book—Marc, Bapu and Nola. I was very, very strategic with my interviews for this book, hence the fact this is a small list. You coloured in perfectly what I needed you to, and brought decades of intellect and experience to topics that aren't easy to write about. I am forever grateful you'd share your insights with me and us all, thank you.

My endorsers. To the unbelievably busy people who read my early manuscript and trusted me enough to throw their name and weight behind me. Your words about my words mean more to me than you'll ever know. Each and every one of you is an inspiration and I feel so privileged to have you standing behind this book. Thank you, thank you, thank you.

Norman. I've had a space on the cover of this book for your endorsement from the time it was just a seed of an idea, because there is no one's opinion—possibly on the planet—I respect more than yours. Thank you for always picking up the phone, making time for me and giving me a start I'll be forever grateful for. Thank you for believing in me and in this.

Karen. Thank you for giving this your expert advocate eye, lending it your 'questions to ask your doctor' which stuck with me from the first time you said it to me, and for being there for me throughout most of my life, including while I was losing Dad. You shaped my early career in ways I'll carry with me always. From the bottom of my heart, to Cannes and back again, thank you.

My supporters. To everyone who has cheered me on, followed me on socials, been on my email list, sent a message, shared a post, made a nice comment in passing or grabbed me at an event or in public to tell me you love what I do—I couldn't be more grateful for you. Taking the time to openly support someone is generous as hell, and it's not lost on me that the vast majority of people don't bother. So, thank you. I never forget the things you say, and am always, always, cheering you on right back.

To all the carers—both personal and professional. You are the best kind of people. Thank you for your open hearts, dedication to humanity and making our world a better place. It might not feel like it in the day-to-day, but your kindness, your nobility—it's having a much bigger impact than you think. To me, you are heroes. Thank you.

Lastly, to Dad. When I told you I was writing this book, even before I had a publisher, you said:

'I'm so delighted our story will be out there, I hope it's a bestseller.'

Nothing will take away the pain of you not being here to enjoy this with me. But I am beyond proud that I can feel you bouncing off every page. Not enough of the world got to know how brilliant you were, I'm hoping this book changes that.

Wherever you are—I hope you know I won the Dad lottery with you. Every time I watch the sun go down I'll think of you and I'll remember. Not just the end, but the magical beginning you gave me and everything in between. I'll never forget your unwavering support, dedication to making the world a better place and most importantly, your undying love for me. I was so, so lucky to be loved by you.

I'll be holding your hand in spirit today and all the days until we meet again.

And oh, the places we'll go.

Resources

The internet can be an overwhelming place. Here, I've curated some of the most valuable digital places to inform, educate and inspire your journey as a carer, patient, clinician or innocent bystander.

Here are some good things to wrap your eyes and ears around.

Read:

- *Tuesdays With Morrie* by Mitch Albom
- *Advice For Future Corpses And Those Who Love Them* by Sallie Tisdale
- *Briefly, Perfectly Human* by Alua Arthur
- *The Good Life* by Bob Waldinger and Marc Schultz
- *Finding Meaning: The Sixth Stage Of Grief* by David Kessler
- *Lost Connections* by Johann Hari
- *Outlive* by Peter Attia
- *So You Think You Know What's Good For You* by Dr Norman Swan
- *Let Them* by Mel Robbins
- *Four Thousand Weeks* by Oliver Burkeman
- *The Resilience Project* by Hugh Van Cuylenburg

Watch:

- *Good Grief* [series] with Dan Levy
- *Dying For Sex* [series] by Nikki Boyer with Michelle Williams
- *What makes a good life? Lessons from the longest study on happiness* [TED talk] Bob Waldinger
- *Why thinking about death helps you live a better life* [TED talk] Alua Arthur
- *What really matters at the end of life* [TED talk] BJ Miller
- *We Don't Move On From Grief, We Move Forward With It* [TED talk] Nora McInerny
- *Voluntary Assisted Dying* [episode] Insight, SBS
- *Ray Martin: The Last Goodbye* [series], SBS
- *The Intouchables* [film]
- *Me Before You* [film]
- *The Theory Of Everything* [film]
- *Still Alice* [film]

Listen:

- The Science & Process of Healing From Grief [podcast episode] *Huberman Lab*
- Why Grief – Like Love – Is Forever [podcast episode] *We Can Do Hard Things*
- *Before We Go* [podcast series] Dr Shoshana Ungerleider
- Grief, Laughter, and Sisterhood: Losing Our Mom and Holding On to Each Other [podcast episode] *Unlocking Us with Brené Brown*
- David Kessler and Brené on Grief and Finding Meaning [podcast episode] *Unlocking Us with Brené Brown*
- *The Secret Life Of Carers* [podcast series] Carers Australia, hosted by Jamila Rizvi

- Dr Emily - Grief Lightning [podcast episode] *The Imperfects*
- *Hold The Moment* [podcast series] Dementia Australia, hosted by Hamish McDonald

Follow:

- Me! @caseyberos
- Good Grief HQ @goodgriefhq (divine people doing good things)
- David Kessler @iamdavidkessler (author and grief thought leader)
- Dr Preeya Alexander @doctor.preeya.alexander (no-nonsense health info)
- End Well @endwellproject (guidance around a good death and everything leading up to it)

Trusted global sources of health information

- **Centers for Disease Control and Prevention (CDC)**
  cdc.gov – US-based health protection agency with up-to-date information on infectious diseases, vaccines and global health issues
- **Harvard Health Publishing**
  health.harvard.edu – evidence-based health advice and medical research from Harvard Medical School
- **Healthline**
  healthline.com – consumer-friendly health content reviewed by medical professionals
- **Johns Hopkins Medicine**
  hopkinsmedicine.org – comprehensive health library and expert guidance from a leading academic medical center
- **Mayo Clinic**
  mayoclinic.org – expert-reviewed information on diseases, symptoms and treatments

- **MedlinePlus**

  medlineplus.gov – reliable health information from the U.S. National Library of Medicine

- **National Health Service (NHS) UK**

  nhs.uk – trusted medical advice, condition guides and treatment options

- **National Institutes of Health (NIH) US**

  nih.gov – America's medical research agency, offering the latest scientific insights

- **World Health Organization (WHO)**

  who.int – global public health information and evidence-based health guidelines

Trusted Australian resources

- **Healthdirect**

  healthdirect.gov.au | 1800 022 222

  Health information, handy symptom checker tool and a 24/7 nurse helpline

- **Better Health Channel**

  betterhealth.vic.gov.au

  Reliable, easy-to-understand health information from the Victorian Government

- **Cancer Australia**

  canceraustralia.gov.au

  National agency providing information on all aspects of cancer prevention, diagnosis, treatment and support

- **Cancer Council**

  cancer.org.au

  Support, advocacy, education and prevention programs for Australians affected by cancer

- **The Heart Foundation**

  heartfoundation.org.au

  Resources for heart disease patients and carers as well as information on heart health checks

- **Dementia Australia**

  dementia.org.au

  Information, education and support for people living with dementia as well as their families. They also have their National Dementia Helpline: 1800 100 500 – 24/7, 365 days a year

- **Beyond Blue**

  beyondblue.org.au

  Support for mental ill-health plus free counselling via phone or online chat

- **Lifeline**

  lifeline.org.au | 13 11 14 – 24/7

  Crisis support for anyone in emotional distress

- **Black Dog Institute**

  blackdoginstitute.org.au

  Mental health resources and digital tools

- **Diabetes Australia**

  diabetesaustralia.com.au

  National body offering advocacy, education and support for people living with all types of diabetes

- **National Diabetes Services Scheme (NDSS)**

  ndss.com.au

  Provides subsidised diabetes products, support and education for Australians with diabetes

- **Asthma Australia**

  asthma.org.au

  Support, education and resources for people with asthma and their carers

- **Lung Foundation Australia**

  lungfoundation.com.au

  Support and information for people with lung diseases including COPD, lung cancer and pulmonary fibrosis

- **Arthritis Australia**

  arthritisaustralia.com.au

  Information and support for managing arthritis and musculoskeletal conditions

- **Stroke Foundation**

  strokefoundation.org.au | 1800 STROKE (1800 787 653)

  Stroke awareness, prevention, recovery and carer support

- **Kidney Health Australia**

  kidney.org.au

  Support and education for people living with kidney disease and those at risk

- **Painaustralia**

  painaustralia.org.au

  Resources and advocacy for people living with chronic pain

- **Quitline**

  quit.org.au | 13 78 48

  Counselling and tools to help Australians quit smoking and vaping

- **Alcohol and Drug Foundation**

  adf.org.au

  Support and prevention resources for alcohol and drug-related harms

For Aboriginal and Torres Strait Islander peoples

- **13YARN**

  13yarn.org.au | 13 92 76 – 24/7 crisis support delivered by Indigenous counsellors

- **Deadly Choices**

  deadlychoices.com.au – health promotion and education initiative empowering Aboriginal and Torres Strait Islander peoples to make healthy choices

- **The Healing Foundation**

  healingfoundation.org.au – supports trauma-aware healing for Stolen Generations survivors and their families

- **National Aboriginal Community Controlled Health Organisation (NACCHO)**

  naccho.org.au – peak body for Aboriginal Community Controlled Health Services

- **Gayaa Dhuwi (Proud Spirit) Australia**

  gayaadhuwi.org.au – social and emotional wellbeing, mental health and suicide prevention for Aboriginal and Torres Strait Islander peoples

- **Australian Indigenous HealthInfoNet**

  healthinfonet.ecu.edu.au – evidence-based information and resources to support health practice and policy

For carers and families

- **Carer Gateway**

  carergateway.gov.au

  Australian Government support service for unpaid carers including counselling, respite, skills training and financial help

- **Aged Care Decisions**

  agedcaredecisions.com.au

  A free service that helps families compare aged care providers and find placements

- **CarerHelp**

  carerhelp.com.au

  Guidance, practical tips and emotional support for carers including for LGBTIQ+ and those living in regional communities

- **Australian Clinical Trials**

  australianclinicaltrials.gov.au

  Search for clinical trials in Australia

- **Health insurance – Department of Health and Aged Care**

  health.gov.au/topics/private-health-insurance/about-private-health-insurance

  Information on how private health insurance works including your rights and what's covered

- **Meal Train**

  mealtrain.com

  A simple online tool for organising meal rosters and support for families going through tough times

- **My Aged Care**

  myagedcare.gov.au

  Your starting point for accessing aged care services in Australia. Check out their searchable directory to compare aged care providers and services in your area

- **OPAN (Older Persons Advocacy Network)**

  opan.org.au

  Free, independent advocacy and support for older people and their families navigating aged care

- **Young Carers Network**

  youngcarersnetwork.com.au

  Information and peer support for young people (aged 25 and under) who provide care for a family member or friend

- **Advance Care Planning Australia**

  advancecareplanning.org.au

  Guides you through the process of documenting your values, wishes and future health care preferences—including free legal forms and how-to help for families

- **CareSearch**

  caresearch.com.au

  Evidence-based palliative care information for people nearing the end of life and those who support them—including carers, families, and health professionals

- **Natural Death Care Centre**

  naturaldeathcarecentre.org

  Education, advocacy and guidance for holistic, natural approaches to death care—including home vigils, death literacy and community support

- **Palliative Care Australia**

  palliativecare.org.au

  National peak body providing information and advocacy on palliative care access, patient rights and end-of-life support

- **Voluntary Assisted Dying – state-based services**

  Search "[Voluntary Assisted Dying] + [your state]"

  Each Australian state has its own laws and processes which are evolving. Visit your state health department website for eligibility and access

- **Zenith Virago – Natural death care and deathwalker training**

  zenithvirago.com

  Workshops, online courses and resources for anyone seeking to deepen their understanding of death, dying and ceremony as well as the in-person deathwalker training I did (and can't recommend highly enough)

Grief and bereavement support

- **Griefline**

  griefline.org.au | 1300 845 745 – 24/7 phone and online support

  Free and confidential support for anyone experiencing grief, loss or trauma, including phone and online counselling

- **Grief Australia**

  grief.org.au

  Grief and bereavement education, counselling and resources for individuals, families and professionals

- **Good Grief HQ**

  goodgriefhq.com

  Modern grief education and support that's honest, inclusive and grounded in lived experience – online programs and workshops as well as grief literacy resources

- **Red Nose Grief and Loss**

  rednosegriefandloss.org.au | 1300 308 307 – 24/7

  Support for families affected by miscarriage, stillbirth, infant or child death – includes counselling, peer support and memorial services

Financial support and planning

- **Carer Gateway – Financial support**

  carergateway.gov.au then search 'financial support'

  Outlines payments and concessions available to unpaid carers, including links to Centrelink and carer allowances

- **Financial Counselling Australia – National Debt Helpline**

  ndh.org.au | 1800 007 007

  Free, independent advice from financial counsellors to help you manage debt, deal with hardship and plan for the future

- **Financial Information Service (FIS)**

  servicesaustralia.gov.au/financial-information-service | 132 300

  A free government service that provides expert advice on pensions, carer allowances, income support and aged care costs

- **MoneySmart – Budget planner and financial tools**

  moneysmart.gov.au

  Practical tools and guidance to help you budget, manage debt, protect your money and plan for unexpected costs

- **My Aged Care**

  myagedcare.gov.au

  Information on government-funded aged care services, including fee structures, financial hardship assistance and subsidies

- **National Disability Insurance Scheme (NDIS)**

  ndis.gov.au

  Provides funding and support to people with disability including carer respite, equipment, home modifications and personal care

References

Introduction

Australian Bureau of Statistics. Disability, Ageing and Carers, Australia: Summary of Findings, 2022 [Internet]. Canberra: ABS; 2024 Jul 4. https://www.abs.gov.au/statistics/health/disability/disability-ageing-and-carers-australia-summary-findings/latest-release#carers

Heyes R, Grimmond D. Economic contribution and sacrifice of carers in New Zealand – November 2022 [Internet]. Wellington: Infometrics; 2022 Nov. https://carers.net.nz/wp-content/uploads/2022/12/Infometrics-Economic-Contribution-of-Caregiving-November-2022-FINAL.pdf

Guardian Life. Caregiving in America [Internet]. New York: Guardian Life; 2023. https://www.guardianlife.com/reports/caregiving-in-america

Carers UK. State of Caring 2022 [Internet]. London: Carers UK; 2022. https://www.carersuk.org/media/ew5e4swg/cuk_state_of_caring_2022_report.pdf

Wildemeersch, D., Jansen, T., Armstrong, P., Miller, N., & Zukes, M. (1997). Strengths and limitations of social learning as a key concept for adult and continuing education in reflexive modernity. In *Crossing borders, breaking boundaries. Research in the education of adults. Proceedings of the 27th Annual Scutrea Conference* (pp. 465–470). University of London, Birckbeck College.

Healthdirect Australia. Preparing for a death at home [Internet].
    Healthdirect. https://www.healthdirect.gov.au/preparing-for-a-
    death-at-home
Carers Australia. Caring Costs Us [Internet]. Carers Australia; 2023.
    https://carersaustralia.com.au/programs-projects/caring-costs-us
Australian Government Department of Health and Aged Care. About
    private health insurance [Internet]. Canberra: DOHAC. https://
    www.health.gov.au/topics/private-health-insurance/about-
    private-health-insurance
Australian Government Department of Health and Aged Care. The
    Australian health system [Internet]. Canberra: DOHAC. https://
    www.health.gov.au/about-us/the-australian-health-system
World Economic Forum. How digital tech can help lower healthcare
    costs [Internet]. Geneva: WEF; 2024 Aug. https://www.weforum
    .org/stories/2024/08/healthcare-costs-digital-tech/
World Health Organization. Health systems performance assessment:
    a roadmap for the future [Internet]. Geneva: WHO; 2024. https://
    www.who.int/publications/i/item/9789240086746
World Economic Forum. Why the care economy is critical for the
    future [Internet]. Geneva: WEF; 2024 May. https://www.weforum
    .org/stories/2024/05/care-economy-future

Chapter 2

NSW Government Asbestos Awareness. When was asbestos
    banned in Australia? [Internet]. Sydney: NSW Government.
    https://www.asbestos.nsw.gov.au/safety/safety-in-the-home/
    when-was-asbestos-banned-in-australia
Asbestos Safety and Eradication Agency. Residential disclosure
    [Internet]. Canberra: ASEA. https://www.asbestossafety.gov.au/
    residentialdisclosure
Australian Institute of Health and Welfare. Cancer data in Australia
    [Internet]. Canberra: AIHW. https://www.aihw.gov.au/reports/
    cancer/cancer-data-in-australia/contents/overview

Mayo Clinic. Mesothelioma: Symptoms and causes [Internet].
Rochester (MN): Mayo Foundation for Medical Education
and Research. https://www.mayoclinic.org/diseases-conditions/
mesothelioma/symptoms-causes

Newman-Toker DE, McDonald KM, Meltzer DO. How much diagnostic safety can we afford, and how should we decide? A health
economics perspective. BMJ Qual Saf. 2013 Oct;22 Suppl
2(Suppl 2):ii11-ii20. doi: 10.1136/bmjqs-2012-001616.

Duckett S. Blood money: paying for pathology services. [Internet].
Melbourne: Grattan Institute; 2016 Feb. https://grattan.edu.au/
wp-content/uploads/2016/02/935-blood-money.pdf

Chapter 3

University of Melbourne. Many Australians are recording their visits
to the doctor – some without permission [Internet]. Melbourne:
University of Melbourne. https://findanexpert.unimelb.edu.au/
news/96375-many-australians-are-recording-their-visits-to-the-
doctor-%E2%80%93-some-without-permission

Shepherd HL, Barratt A, Trevena LJ, McGeechan K, Carey K,
Epstein RM, Butow PN, Del Mar CB, Entwistle V, Tattersall MH.
Three questions that patients can ask to improve the quality of
information physicians give about treatment options: a cross-over
trial. Patient Educ Couns. 2011 Sep;84(3):379-85. doi: 10.1016/j
.pec.2011.07.022.

Australian Government. My Aged Care [Internet]. Canberra:
Australian Government. https://www.myagedcare.gov.au/

National Disability Insurance Scheme. About the NDIS [Internet].
Canberra: NDIS. https://www.ndis.gov.au/

Chapter 4

U.S. Drug Enforcement Administration. Fentanyl [Internet].
Washington, D.C.: DEA. https://www.dea.gov/factsheets/fentanyl

Chapter 5

Robbins M. *Let them*. US: Hay House LLC. Mel Robbins
Productions; 2023.

Waldinger R, Schulz M. *The good life: Lessons from the world's longest
scientific study of happiness*. New York: Simon & Schuster; 2023.

Chapter 6

Liu Z, Heffernan C, Tan J. Caregiver burden: A concept analysis. Int
J Nurs Sci. 2020;7(4):438-445. doi: 10.1016/j.ijnss.2020.07.012.

Cleveland Clinic. Caregiver burnout [Internet]. Cleveland (OH):
Cleveland Clinic. https://my.clevelandclinic.org/health/diseases/
9225-caregiver-burnout

Kiecolt-Glaser JK, Marucha PT, Malarkey WB, Mercado AM, Glaser R.
Slowing of wound healing by psychological stress. Lancet. 1995
Nov 4;346(8984):1194-6. doi: 10.1016/s0140-6736(95)92899-5.

Chapter 7

Harvard University. Harvard Study of Adult Development [Internet].
Cambridge (MA): Harvard University. https://news.harvard.edu/
gazette/story/2017/04/over-nearly-80-years-harvard-study-has-
been-showing-how-to-live-a-healthy-and-happy-life/

Coan JA, Schaefer HS, Davidson RJ. Lending a hand: social
regulation of the neural response to threat. Psychol Sci. 2006
Dec;17(12):1032-9. doi: 10.1111/j.1467-9280.2006.01832.x.

Chapter 8

Western Australian Department of Health. Overview of the process:
Voluntary assisted dying [Internet]. Perth: Western Australian
Department of Health. https://www.health.wa.gov.au/-/media/Corp/
Documents/Health-for/Voluntary-assisted-dying/Overview-of-the-
Process.pdf

Brockie J. Voluntary assisted dying [Internet]. Sydney: SBS Insight.
https://www.sbs.com.au/ondemand/news-series/insight/
insight-2020/insight-s2020-ep5/1699323459507

Chapter 10

Virago Z. *The Deathwalker Training*. Brunswick Heads (NSW): Natural Death Care Centre; 2025 Jan.

Becker C, Lecheler L, Hochstrasser S, et al. Association of Communication Interventions to Discuss Code Status With Patient Decisions for Do-Not-Resuscitate Orders: A Systematic Review and Meta-analysis. *JAMA Netw Open*. 2019;2(6):e195033. doi:10.1001/jamanetworkopen.2019.5033

Chapter 11

Australian Government Department of Social Services. Financial support for carers [Internet]. Canberra: Department of Social Services. https://www.carergateway.gov.au/help-and-support/caring-me/available-support-carers/financial-support

World Population Review. Medical bankruptcies by country 2025 [Internet]. World Population Review. https://worldpopulation review.com/country-rankings/medical-bankruptcies-by-country

Becker G, Murphy K, Philipson T. The value of life near its end and terminal care [Internet]. Cambridge (MA): National Bureau of Economic Research; 2007 Aug. (Working Paper No. 13333). https://www.nber.org/papers/w13333

Australian Government. The physical process of dying [brochure]. Canberra: Healthdirect Australia.

Department of Health, Palliative Care Australia. About the process of dying [flyer]. Canberra: Australian Government.

Government of Western Australia Department of Health. Prepare to care handbook: a resource for family and friend carers. Perth: Carers WA.

Chapter 14

Kessler D. *Finding meaning: The sixth stage of grief*. New York: Scribner; 2019.

Brown B. *Atlas of the heart: Mapping meaningful connection and the language of human experience*. New York: Random House; 2021.

Huberman A. Dr. Gabor Maté: Understanding & healing trauma [Internet]. Huberman Lab Podcast; 2023 Sep 11. http://youtube.com/watch?v=dzOvi0Aa2EA

Maté G. *The Myth of Normal: Trauma, Illness, and Healing in a Toxic Culture*. New York: Avery; 2022.

Laozi. *Tao Te Ching*. Translated by Mitchell S. New York: Harper Perennial Modern Classics; 2006.

Tisdale S. *Advice for future corpses (and those who love them)*. New York: Touchstone; 2018.

Neimeyer RA. Meaning reconstruction in bereavement: Development of a research program. *Death Stud*. 2019;43(2):79–91. doi: 10.1080/07481187.2018.1456620.

Australian Institute of Health and Welfare. The last year of life: patterns in health service use and expenditure [Internet]. Canberra: AIHW. https://www.aihw.gov.au/reports/life-expectancy-deaths/the-last-year-of-life-health-service-use-patterns/contents/key-findings

Australian Institute of Health and Welfare. International health data comparisons [Internet]. Canberra: AIHW. https://www.aihw.gov.au/reports/international-health-data-comparisons

Harvard Health Publishing. How to talk to children about the serious illness of a loved one [Internet]. Boston: Harvard Medical School; 2019 Dec 2. https://www.health.harvard.edu/blog/how-to-talk-to-children-about-the-serious-illness-of-a-loved-one-2019120218468

Chapter 15

Robbins M. Don't learn this too late: Make an authentic life now, by getting real about the end [Internet]. The Mel Robbins Podcast; 2024 Oct 31. https://www.melrobbins.com/episode/episode-229

Chapter 16

Sheridan T, creator. *1883* [television series]. United States: Paramount+; 2021–2022

Printed and bound by CPI Group (UK) Ltd, Croydon, CR0 4YY

06/08/2025

14714618-0001